Overview Guide to Learning Piano: From Piano Method to Level 8

Jamie Mellway and Adrian Charles Preston

Contents

Introduction

Are you someone who has dreamt of mastering the piano but found yourself discouraged by the complexities of the piano path? Perhaps you've been eager to embark on a musical journey but felt overwhelmed by the various piano methods, conservatory programs, technical exercises, and supplemental books. Maybe you found the various programs of structured curriculum, graded levels (exams), and diverse repertoire intimidating. If so, fear not because this book is designed specifically for you. It serves as your beacon of clarity amidst the musical labyrinth, offering a roadmap to navigate the challenges of the piano journey with confidence and ease. Say goodbye to confusion and hello to a world where playing beautiful pieces and achieving your musical aspirations are within reach. Get ready to embark on a transformative journey from piano enthusiast to accomplished pianist.

The piano journey usually begins with a piano method. These progressive programs start from zero and prepare you for later conservatory programs. Here you learn the basics of reading sheet music, technique, rhythm, scales and chords, and musical expression. After a year or so with a piano method, one is ready to make the transition to a conservatory program.

There are several conservatory programs, but this book will focus on the Royal Conservatory of Music (RCM) piano program. This program stands as a hallmark of excellence in music education. Its structured curriculum ensures a systematic development of skills, from foundational concepts to advanced techniques. The graded levels, marked by exams, provide clear milestones for progress, motivating pianists to strive for continuous improvement. Moreover, the diverse repertoire offered by the RCM program allows pianists to explore a wide range of musical styles and genres, enriching their musical experience and versatility.

Despite its esteemed reputation and the numerous benefits it offers, the RCM program can seem daunting, especially for adults returning to the instrument. As we have personally navigated this journey, we understand the challenges that arise, from grappling with complex musical concepts to managing performance anxiety. These experiences have shaped our understanding of the program and inspired us to create this guide, bridging the gap between aspiration and achievement in piano education.

This book aims to empower aspiring pianists like you to approach the RCM program with confidence and enthusiasm. It demystifies the complexities of the program, providing clear explanations, practical tips, and strategies to succeed at each stage. Whether you're starting your musical journey or aiming for higher levels of achievement, this book equips you with the knowledge and tools needed to excel in the RCM program.

Structured into three parts, the book offers a comprehensive approach to mastering the piano program and exploring broader musical horizons.

Part 1 delves into understanding the piano program deeply. Here, we cover the curriculum in detail, including insights into repertoire selection, technical requirements, and exam expectations. This part provides a solid foundation for navigating the intricacies of the program with confidence, ensuring that you understand the core elements required for success.

In Part 2, we focus on progressing through the levels, offering a detailed breakdown by level. This part is designed to guide you through the specific challenges and skills required at each level, along with strategies for effective practice, performance preparation, and exam success. Whether you're tackling a piano method or aiming for the highest RCM levels, Part 2 provides the guidance you need to navigate each stage successfully and achieve your musical goals.

Finally, Part 3 takes you beyond the RCM curriculum to explore other musical interests. This part encourages you to broaden your musical horizons beyond the classical repertoire and strictly solo piano music. Here we look at chord-based music, music from bands and ensembles, and different genres. Helping you enrich your overall musical experience and discover new avenues for creative expression.

As we conclude this introduction, we invite you to embark on this exciting journey with us as your guide. Let's navigate the intricacies of the piano program together, unlock the secrets of musical mastery, and discover the joy of making music to its fullest. Are you ready to take the first step toward musical excellence? Let's begin.

Chapter 1

Welcome to the RCM Piano Journey

I—Adrian—remember that since I was a child, I was always interested in the piano; I heard its notes, and my soul vibrated, maybe because my mother was fond of it and often heard beautiful classical works when I was in her womb. Some of them became my favorites, like Prelude in C Major by J. S. Bach, Nocturnes by F. Chopin, and Moonlight Sonata by Beethoven.

A little late for the recommended standards, I started to receive private lessons of my favorite instrument at the age of 12. However, by the time I was 15, I grew bored of the monotonous teaching methods. My friends were forming rock bands and exploring modern music, which I found more exciting but not present in my piano lessons. Consequently, I stopped taking lessons.

So, I abandoned this practice for more than three years and opted to try the electric bass first and then the guitar. Afterward, I wandered through some garages of my classmates... but my great love was the piano.

After a while, I felt again the need to resume its practice, but from another, more complete perspective, I wanted to explore higher levels of teaching. That is how I became interested in the RCM method, which I got to know through a new fellow student who was a participant in it, although he played the cello and seemed very pleased.

I decided to hire a qualified teacher in the system and started studying with high expectations. The first few months, I felt very comfortable, but gradually, I began to feel frustrated, as I found the system a bit dense, repetitive, and overwhelming.

Could it be that I didn't understand the learning program? Perhaps it was a program that didn't adapt to my needs and expectations. Do you, my dear reader, have the same questions that assailed me at that time?

Perhaps many people identified with or are in the same position I was in, so I embarked on a deep research process, and this guide is premised on demystifying the RCM program in its entirety to answer all possible uncertainties.

Now I—Jamie—did not get as far. I started with a chord-first approach as a teenager learning from a teacher without any books that gave me a quick start to play in a band and write music with a MIDI sequencer.

Later as an adult, I had worked through the *Faber* and *Faber Adult Piano Adventures* books with a teacher and was just starting the Royal Conservatory of Music program. Things seemed to be going well until I got to the RCM Baroque repertoire where I hit a wall and then started losing interest.

At this point, I just wanted someone to give me an overview of the conservatory program, so I knew what I was signing up for. I knew what the minimal requirements were for passing the tests, but I wanted to know what a typical, full program was. This would include all the extra books needed and what scales and exercises would be done in each grade/level. I knew things like jazz and pop music weren't big parts of the conservatory program and wanted to know if the program could be supplemented to add those things in.

I wasn't getting the answers from the teachers I was asking as I think they thought I was trying to cheap out and not have a piano teacher anymore. We were not able to get past the Baroque wall, so I stopped playing the piano and instead focused on the theory rudiments exams. Afterward, I stopped lessons altogether. Perhaps I would have continued playing if I switched to the kids 3A level piano method books or *Christopher Norton Connections* and waited until my sight-reading and left-hand control were better to handle the Baroque pieces.

It also might just be that the conservatory program was not for me. In any case, the piano remained in the back of my mind as a thing I had something to say about. When I started getting interested in publishing, this quickly came to the forefront, and we began working on this book together. We hope our combined experience brings something to this topic.

Introduction to the RCM Program, Its History and Philosophy

The Royal Conservatory of Music, located in Toronto, Canada, is one of the largest and most prestigious music education institutions in the world. With more than 130 years of history, it was founded in 1886 by Edward Fisher, a young American organist. Initially, it was called the Toronto Conservatory of Music, and in 1947 King George VI gave it its royal designation.

Over the years, it has been a beacon of excellence in musical training, setting the highest standards with its elaborate curriculum and its formidable line-up of artists, many of whom are internationally acclaimed, among the most prominent of whom we can name:

- Oscar Peterson: Grammy and Juno award-winning pianist and composer

- Sarah McLachlan: Grammy and Juno award-winning singer and composer

- Teresa Stratas: Grammy Award-winning opera singer

- Sir Roger Norrington: Internationally renowned conductor

- Glenn Gould: Legendary pianist, composer, writer, and broadcaster

These talented stars have left a significant mark on the global music scene; they are a testament to the high level of training offered by the Royal Conservatory of Music.

The pedagogical and philosophical approach of this prestigious conservatory is based on the belief that music and the arts are fundamental to personal growth, and these disciplines can be a bridge that connects humanity by developing its potential.

In addition, the conservatory offers programs in dance, theater, and visual arts, providing a comprehensive arts education to its students. Through these programs, they have the opportunity to explore different forms of expression and develop a deeper understanding of how the arts can enrich our lives.

While it is an institution that has been operating for years, it has always been and remained at the top. This is thanks to its structured teaching program that, at first, may seem somewhat confusing and intimidating, but explained in the right way, is easy to understand.

Advantages of Structured Learning Through the RCM Program

There are many advantages of studying and training using this program, some of which are:

- It is a structured plan that focuses on providing its students with blended learning so that they have comprehensive training.

- It also focuses on technique, providing the student with excellent finger dexterity, coordination, power, and control, which results in a high level of virtuosity, allowing the same to dabble in various styles of music if desired.

- Musicality, expression, dynamics, artistry, and phrasing.

- Auditory skills that develop rhythmic precision.

- It is effectively sequenced, so each student learns at their own pace and scales level by level in the appropriate manner toward achieving their goals.

- The student can take the classes face-to-face at the physical institution in downtown Toronto or remotely with a private teacher.

- Digital educational tools verified by leading North American educators.

- Emphasis on student development and creativity.

- Varied and appropriate repertoire for each level.

- It can be taken by children as well as adults of any age.

- One of the most important benefits that have made RCM such a highly valued method is its system of evaluations, which are conducted by renowned musicians and give the student a sense of accomplishment that allows them to develop confidence in their performance.

- The program also has a very interesting feature for high school students, as they can earn a grade 11 music credit for completing and passing RCM level 7 and a grade 12 credit for completing and passing level 8.

Among the advantages of the RCM program, we can't forget the support given to teachers who want to be part of this teaching method through online courses that provide the most complete pedagogical preparation, where graduates will have a summative portfolio and receive a certificate of successful completion of the course that accredits them as certified teachers.

Students and teachers, with the permanent support of the conservatory, form a harmonious community where the pride of belonging to it prevails.

Different Options Within the RCM Program

The RCM program is structured at different levels, which allows students to progress at their own pace. Each level represents a set of skills and knowledge that must be mastered before advancing to the next.

Throughout this process, you will receive different certificates according to your ability, as shown below:

- preparatory A and B. levels 1–4. Elementary certificates
- levels 5–8. Intermediate certificates
- levels 9–10. Advanced certificates

The pros of this option are:

- step-by-step learning, ensuring that students fully master one level before moving on to the next
- providing a clear structure and progression path, which can be motivating for students

Cons:

- Some students may find the pace of progression daunting if they find a level particularly challenging.
- Students may feel pressured to move quickly through the levels, which can result in a superficial understanding of skills and knowledge.

Also, the RCM offers exams on an optional basis at each level (i.e., they can be taken directly without having taken the exams at the previous levels). However, it should be noted that this only applies up to level 8, and subsequent levels cannot be skipped.

The pros we can take into account are:

- It provides an objective assessment of the student's skills and knowledge.
- It offers students a clear objective for their study and practice.

On the other hand, the cons are that some students may find the exam experience stressful and demanding beyond their expectations.

In addition to the certifications awarded for levels passed, the RCM offers alternative certification programs that represent the pinnacle of achievement within the program. These are the ARCT and LRCM diplomas.

Students may apply for the Associate Diploma exam upon completion of the level 10 practical exam and all prerequisite theory exams (*Curriculum and Disciplines*, n.d.). This exam consists of a complete recital of up to 60 minutes.

Let's review the pros:

- Provides top-level recognition both nationally and internationally.
- It opens doors at the artistic and academic levels.

And let's also look at the cons:

- It requires a high commitment of time, effort, and dedication.
- The preparation to reach such a level and to be able to successfully pass the tests requires at least one year of thorough preparation.

It is important to choose the RCM program option that best suits your individual goals and learning style. Here are some considerations you might want to keep in mind:

If your goal is simply to enjoy music and play the piano for pleasure, you may opt for a less structured and more flexible path within the program.

If you have aspirations of becoming a professional musician, you may need to follow a more structured and rigorous path, studying each level and taking the corresponding exams.

The itinerary for adults may vary in time and form with children or teenagers, either because they have a broader experience playing the piano, which would positively impact the progress of their studies, being able to accelerate the progression in the levels.

The RCM program, from its foundation to the present, has sought to provide its students with the best tools for musical learning. It has become a flagship in the training of artists in all its facets, both personal self-realization and internationally renowned musicians, through its structured system.

In the next chapters, we'll dive into a demystification of its curriculum so students who wish to follow this system can do so without any fear.

Let's keep moving forward and learning more about this wonderful program!

Part I

The RCM Program—Demystifying the Curriculum

This part consists of 6 chapters, each one focused on demystifying the RCM program curriculum.

We will start with navigating and understanding its broad repertoire, providing suggestions for effective performance in it.

Then we'll explain the purpose of technical studies, providing suggestions and offering guidance on how to practice them. You'll have a deep insight of the art of études and how they help you develop your skills perfectly.

You will be introduced to fundamental concepts of music theory and the importance of mastering them. Followed by the development of musical skills that can be acquired, such as sight-reading.

And finally, you'll learn how to embark on the RCM program, find a suitable teacher and clear up insecurities.

Chapter 2

Repertoire—A Journey Through the Musical Options of the RCM

Imagine a musical journey filled with exhilarating challenges and moments of pure joy. Selecting the right RCM repertoire is the first step to getting there. This chapter helps you navigate the basic components of the RCM piano curriculum, allowing you to choose pieces that will not only develop your skills but also ignite your musical passion.

Demystifying RCM Repertoire Lists

The RCM repertoire lists may seem overwhelming at first, but once you understand their basic structure, they become much more manageable. These lists are organized by levels, each representing a set of musical skills and knowledge. Within each grade/level, you will find a variety of genres and categories, from Baroque music to contemporary compositions.

Each genre and category has its own selection criteria, which are based on factors such as technical complexity, musical style, and the historical period of the piece. For example, a Baroque piece may require a different approach in terms of phrasing and ornamentation than a piece from the Romantic period.

This is where the role of teachers becomes crucial; they can help students navigate these lists, guiding them to pieces that not only are appropriate for their skill level but also align with their musical interests. They can provide guidance on how to approach the technical demands of a piece, how to interpret its musical style, and how to understand it in the context of its historical period.

The RCM establishes a set of criteria that students must meet for each level of their piano program. It is important to know and understand each of these for effective performance.

- **Technical demands:** Each level of the program requires a certain degree of technical ability. This may include the ability to play scales, arpeggios, chords, and other technical patterns with accuracy and fluency. As students advance through the levels, these demands become more complex.

- **Musical style:** Students must demonstrate an understanding and effective application of musical styles. This may involve interpretation of dynamics, phrasing, articulation, and other elements that are characteristic of a given musical style.

- **Historical period:** The pieces in the RCM repertoire span a wide range of historical periods, from Baroque to Contemporary. Students should be able to perform each in a manner that is appropriate for each period.

These concepts are fundamental to the development of a well-rounded and versatile pianist. When preparing for an RCM exam, students should consider how each piece in their repertoire relates to these areas.

Creating a Balanced Repertoire

A balanced repertoire is one that integrates compositions from various musical styles, periods, and technical challenges. It offers multiple benefits:

- Exposure to a variety of musical styles, such as Baroque, classical, romantic, and contemporary, immersing you in diverse musical voices and aesthetics. This can enhance understanding and appreciation of music.

- Exposure to compositions from different historical eras, giving you the opportunity to understand how music has evolved over time. This can provide valuable insight into how historical and cultural events have shaped it.

- A versatile skill set can be developed. Practicing various techniques, such as scales, arpeggios, articulation, and phrasing, can contribute to improved technique and musical interpretation.

In addition, it is relevant to mention the concept of *comfort zone*. While it may be tempting to remain in what you know and what you have mastered, going beyond that zone is essential for growth. By exploring new compositions, styles, and techniques, one can discover new facets of music and of oneself as a musician.

Also, it is important to note that a balanced repertoire can help develop adaptability, as each musical style and historical era requires a different interpretive approach. In addition, facing new technical challenges can strengthen your resilience and ability to overcome obstacles. In short, a balanced repertoire not only enriches the musical experience but also fosters personal and artistic growth.

Choosing pieces for repertoire at the Royal Conservatory of Music should be an informed and thoughtful process. It is essential to select pieces that match your skill level and personal interests, always keeping in mind your teacher's recommendations.

Choosing pieces that do not match your level can result in frustration and discouragement. On the other hand, choosing pieces below that level may not provide the challenge necessary for development. Therefore, it is crucial to find a balance at the time of selection that provides the right degree of challenge.

Another factor to consider is your personal preferences for musical styles and composers. Music is a form of individual expression, so it is important that the pieces chosen resonate with the vibration of each soul.

So, as you can see, choosing pieces for a good repertoire should be an informed process in which a wide variety of factors should be taken into account: skill level, technical demands, personal preferences, and emotional connection. By making the right selection, your repertoire will be both challenging and rewarding.

Musical Styles of the RCM

Baroque Music

Baroque music, which spans from 1600 to 1750 in the classical musical tradition of Western Europe, presents unique challenges for pianists. Unlike modern music, which often relies heavily on chordal harmony, Baroque music employs counterpoint—a technique that interweaves multiple independent melodies simultaneously. This intricate texture demands a different approach to playing and interpreting the music.

In the works of Johann Sebastian Bach, for example, the melody can appear in either hand o r both hands simultaneously, requiring pianists to develop a high level of independence and dexterity. Bach's music grows increasingly complex as students progress, with pieces that often incorporate three or four simultaneous melodies. These intricate contrapuntal structures are like puzzles, with each voice maintaining its own melodic and rhythmic integrity while contributing to the overall harmony. This melodic richness is a hallmark of Baroque music and provides pianists with the opportunity to refine their technical and interpretative skills.

The main Baroque composer is Bach and his works are central to piano education and performance. The Notebook for Anna Magdalena Bach (Notenbuch der Anna Magdalena Bach) includes pieces by various composers, featuring easier pieces that were popular with Bach's family. A particularly recognizable piece from this collection is Christian Petzold's Minuet in G Major (Grade 3). Selections from the Notebook appear in List A of every grade from 1 to 6 in the RCM curriculum.

Intermediate piano introduces Bach's two part inventions and three part inventions in Grade 7-9. These pieces help students develop contrapuntal playing skills. Bach originally wrote the Inventions to teach composition and considered them pedagogically essential. These lead to the Preludes and Fugues from The Well-Tempered Clavier in Grade 10. They represent the pinnacle of Bach's contrapuntal writing, demanding both technical proficiency and interpretive insight.

In Grade 10 and ARCT, students encounter Bach's English Suites, French Suites, and Partitas for Keyboard. Many of the pieces at lower grades (4-8) are selections from these suites.

Movements from the Capriccio on the Departure of a Beloved Brother (Grade 9 and 10), pieces from the Notebook for Wilhelm Friedemann Bach (Grades 6, 8, 9), and the Overture in the French Style (Grade 7) are also included in the RCM curriculum. There is also a

Minuet from Suite in G Minor (2), a Allemande (5), Little Preludes (5-8), a Prelude (6), and Fugue (9).

ARCT also includes Chromatic Fantasia and Fugue in D Minor, Fantasia and Fugue in A Minor, Italian Concerto, Suite in A Minor, and several Toccata. In Grade 10 and ARCT, List A exclusively features works by J.S. Bach, ensuring that students at these levels gain comprehensive exposure to his music.

Other big baroque piano composers are Handel and Scarlatti. Many of the pieces from grades 5 to 9 are selections from Handel's Suites. Every Scarlatti piece in the RCM program is a Sonata, known for their technical brilliance and expressive depth.

Classical Music

The Classical period, which spans from 1750–1825, is a fascinating time in music history. We often use the term *classical music* to refer to everything before the beginning of the 20th century, but in reality, it has a more specific meaning. One of the most important innovations during this period was the development of the piano.

While the first prototypes of pianos were tested in Bach's later years, it was during the Romantic period when the piano acquired its current form. This versatile and expressive instrument became a favorite of composers and musicians.

In the Classical period, three composers stand out for their influence and legacy:

- Joseph Haydn, known as the *Father of the Symphony*: Haydn was a master of symphonic form and chamber music. His symphonies and string quartets are masterful examples of classical elegance and structure.

- Wolfgang Amadeus Mozart: A musical prodigy from an early age, Mozart composed an astonishing amount of works in his short life. His operas, symphonies, and concerts are masterpieces filled with grace and beauty.

- Ludwig van Beethoven: Beethoven is the bridge between Classicism and Romanticism. His symphonies, like the famous "Symphony No. 9," are monumental and emotional. Beethoven challenged conventions and opened new musical possibilities.

Although Haydn, Mozart, and Beethoven are the pillars of the Classical period, there were also other notable composers. Exploring their works allows us to appreciate the diversity and beauty of this musical era.

Many of the classical pieces, from Grades 3 to 8, are sonatinas and there are also some of the easier sonatas. The advanced grades are almost exclusively sonatas. Many of the early pieces are dance forms such as minuets, gavottes, and German dances.

Romantic Music

Romantic music, which spanned approximately between the years 1810 and 1910, was a period in which composers sought to express deep and personal emotions through their works. These compositions are characterized by reflecting intense feelings of love, sadness, passion, and melancholy. During this period, music was seen as an independent art with great possibilities of expression, and romantic musicians as virtuosos capable of connecting the masses with this spiritual world through their works.

Among the most outstanding pianists of this period are:

- Frédéric Chopin was a Polish pianist and composer widely recognized as one of the most important musicians of Romanticism. He is especially known for his pieces written for piano, excelling in genres such as the nocturne, the waltz, and the polonaise. His music, which was often inspired by popular songs from Poland, created a unique fusion between nationalism and romanticism.

- Franz Liszt was a Hungarian virtuoso pianist and composer. He is known for his dramatic and technically challenging works. His compositions, such as the Hungarian Rhapsodies, Liebesträume, and various études (including the Transcendental Études), pushed the boundaries of piano technique. Most of his works in the RCM are at the advanced levels with Consolation No. 1 in level 8.

- Clara Schumann (1819-1896) was one of the most distinguished pianists of her time. She was renowned for her technical skill, interpretative depth, and the emotional intensity of her performances. Clara played a significant role in promoting the works of her husband, Robert Schumann, and other contemporaries such as Johannes Brahms.

Modern Music—Classical

Modern classical music has experienced a significant evolution, characterized by a diversification of styles and the breaking of traditional musical boundaries. Throughout the 20th century and into the 21st, composers such as Claude Debussy, Dmitri Kabalevsky, and Igor Stravinsky emerged, revolutionizing the rules of music and expanding the possibilities of musical expression.

- Claude Debussy (1862-1918): Often associated with the Impressionist movement, Debussy's music is known for its innovative use of harmony, texture, and color. His compositions, such as "Clair de Lune" and "Prélude à l'après-midi d'un faune," broke away from traditional tonality and explored new scales and modes, creating a more fluid and atmospheric sound. Debussy's work paved the way for many modern composers who sought to push the boundaries of classical music.

- Dmitri Kabalevsky (1904-1987): Kabalevsky was a prominent Soviet composer who made significant contributions to music education. His piano works, such as "Children's Pieces, Op. 27" and "Twenty-Four Preludes," are noted for their melodic appeal and pedagogical value. Kabalevsky's music often incorporates folk elements and accessible themes, making his study books particularly attractive for young pianists. However, these pieces are also suitable for adults who appreciate their lyrical and rhythmic qualities.

- Igor Stravinsky (1882-1971): Stravinsky is renowned for his innovative and often controversial compositions that span various styles, including primitivism, neoclassicism, and serialism. Works like "The Rite of Spring," "Petrushka," and "The Firebird" showcase his ability to blend complex rhythms, dissonant harmonies, and dynamic orchestration. Stravinsky's influence on modern classical music is profound, as he continuously challenged the conventions of the genre and inspired subsequent generations of composers.

In the modern classical era, composers enjoyed creating study books with attractive pieces for children. These educational works often feature engaging melodies and accessible technical challenges designed to develop young musicians' skills. Notable examples include Kabalevsky's "Children's Pieces, Op. 27" and Béla Bartók's "Mikrokosmos," a collection of progressive piano pieces that introduce various technical and musical concepts.

Although labeled as works for children, these pieces are also suitable for adults, offering valuable technical exercises and opportunities for musical exploration. The appeal of these works lies in their ability to combine educational value with artistic expression, making them a staple in the repertoire of both young and mature pianists.

Preparatory Levels and Piano Methods

Before progressing to RCM Level 1, it is essential to establish a solid foundation in piano basics. This foundational knowledge is typically gained through various piano methods and the preparatory levels of the RCM. Among the most popular piano methods for adults are Alfred's Basic Adult Piano Course series and Faber and Faber's Adult Piano Adventures series. These methods are designed to cater to adult learners, providing a structured and engaging approach to learning piano.

Typically, adult beginners will work through Books 1 and 2 of one of these series, which cover the essential skills needed to build a strong musical foundation. These books are comprehensive, offering lessons that introduce the fundamentals of piano playing in a progressive manner. Upon completion of these books, students are usually ready to transition to RCM Level 1. The RCM's Preparatory A and B books complement these adult piano methods, reinforcing and expanding on the concepts learned in Books 1 and 2.

In these early stages, piano methods focus on several key areas of music education. One of the primary objectives is to teach students how to read music. This is achieved by using landmarks and intervals, which help learners quickly identify notes and understand their relationships on the staff. Additionally, students are introduced to basic playing techniques, such as staccato and legato, which are essential for creating different articulations and expressions in their playing.

Another critical component is learning the basic terminology for dynamics and tempo. Understanding terms like "forte" and "piano" (loud and soft), as well as tempo markings like "allegro" and "andante" (fast and slow), is crucial for interpreting music accurately. Hand positions and fingerings are also emphasized to ensure that students develop proper technique and avoid bad habits that can hinder their progress.

Rhythm and meters are fundamental elements covered in these early levels. Students learn to recognize and play different note values and time signatures, which are essential for maintaining a steady pulse and understanding the structure of music. Additionally, they are introduced to slurs and phrases, which help in understanding musical sentences and shaping their playing with musicality and expression.

By mastering these foundational concepts through the structured lessons of Alfred's and Faber and Faber's methods, along with the complementary RCM Preparatory books, students build a robust technical and musical foundation. This preparation ensures a smooth transition to RCM Level 1, where they can continue to develop their skills and tackle more complex repertoire.

RCM Levels

The RCM has 10 different levels, each with an extensive piano repertoire, but in this book, we will only cover levels from 1–8.

- Level 1: This level includes simple, short pieces that allow students to become familiar with the instrument and develop basic skills such as note reading and finger technique.

- Level 2–3: These levels include pieces of greater difficulty and length, requiring more technical control and musicality on the part of the student. More advanced concepts, such as the use of pedals and dynamics, are introduced.

- Level 4–5: At these levels, students begin to tackle more technically challenging repertoire, requiring greater control of dynamics, articulation, and musical interpretation. Works by classical and romantic composers are included, as well as contemporary works.

- Level 6–8: Reaching the pinnacle of difficulty, students tackle a repertoire of greater technical and musical complexity, requiring a high level of skill and dexterity on the piano.

Below are some repertoire suggestions for each level, according to the RCM Piano Syllabus:

Level 1

Recommended repertoire:

List A: Baroque and classical repertoire

- Bach, Johann Sebastian—Chorale, BWV 514 (in Notenbuch der Anna Magdalena Bach BAR; WIE)

- Graupner, Christoph—Bourrée in D Minor (in Notebook for Wolfgang)

List B: Romantic repertoire, 20th and 21st centuries

- Glover, David Carr—Blinky the Robot (in Belwin Contest Winners, 2 ALF)

- Humbert, Georges Frank—The Chocolate Automaton (in Piano Piccolo OTT)

List C: Inventions

- Duke, David Gordon, arr—She's Like the Swallow (in Music of Our Time, 2 WAT)
- Kenins, George Juris, arr—Invention on a Latvian folk tune KNS

Level 2

Recommended repertoire:

List A: Baroque and classical repertoire

- Beethoven—Echoes in G Major, WoO 23
- J. S. Bach—Minuet in G Major

List B: Romantic, 20th and 21st century repertoire

- Rossi—Desert of Atacama
- Case—Waltz of the Shadows

List C: Inventions

- Christopher—Invention in C Major
- Gallant—In Canoe

Level 3

Recommended repertoire:

List A: Baroque repertoire

- Bourée in A Minor—Krieger
- Bach, Johann Sebastian, attr.—Musette in D Major, BWV Anh. 126 (in Notenbuch der Anna Magdalena Bach BAR; WIE)

List B: Classical and classical-style repertoire

- Hüllmandel, Nicolas-Joseph—Allegro in G Major, op. 5, no. 5 (in OTT Piano Piccolo)
- Mozart, Wolfgang Amadeus—Minuet in D Major, K 7

List C: Romantic, 20th and 21st century repertoire

- Bennett, Rhonda—Holiday Parade (in Myklas Contest Winners, 2 ALF)
- Jinga, Naina—Circus Waltz JIN

Level 4

Recommended repertoire:

List A: Baroque repertoire

- Bach, Johann Sebastian—Musette, from the English Suite no. 3 in G Minor, BWV 808
- Scarlatti, Domenico—Sonata in D Minor, K 32

List B: Classical and classical style repertoire

- Beethoven, Ludwig van—German Dance in E-flat Major (no. 9)
- Mozart, Leopold—Menuett in A Major (no. 9)

List C: Romantic, 20th and 21st century repertoire

- Donkin, Christine—Good Times DKN
- Pettigrew, Laura—Pack Ice PTW

Level 5

Recommended repertoire:

List A: Baroque repertoire

- Bach, Johann Sebastian—Allemande in G Minor, BWV 836
- Graupner, Christoph—Intrada in C Major (in Piano Baroque ALF)

List B: Classical and classical style repertoire

- Cimarosa, Domenico—Sonata in G Minor, C 33 (in Haydn-Mozart- Cimarosa: Leichte Klavierstücke WIE)
- Mozart, Leopold—Notebook for Nannerl—Allegro moderato in F Major

List C: Romantic repertoire, 20th and 21st century

- Copland, Aaron—Sunday Afternoon Music (in Masters of Our Time, 1 FIS)
- Hansen, Joan—Traffic (in Music of Our Time, 5 WAT)

Level 6

Recommended repertoire:

List A: Baroque repertoire

- Scarlatti, Domenico—Sonata in G Major
- Seixas, José Antonio Carlos de—Toccata in C Minor (no. 8 in Early Portuguese Music for Keyboard, 1 OTT)

List B: Classical and classical style repertoire

- Hook, James Sonatina—in D Major, op. 12, no. 1 1 1st movement

- Lichner, Heinrich Sonatina—in G Major, op. 4, no. 3 KJO; SCH 1 last movement: Rondo

List C: Repertoire of the Romantic, 20th and 21st centuries

- Assiginaak, Barbara u—Miimii (Mourning Dove) AGK

- Beach, Amy—Children's Carnival, op. 25 HIL 1 Secrets (no. 5)

Level 7

Recommended repertoire:

List A: Baroque repertoire

- Kirnberger, Johann Philipp—Recueil d'airs de danse caractéristiques 1 Passepied in D Major (no. 8)

- Rameau, Jean-Philippe—Pièces de clavecin (1724) 1 La joyeuse.

List B: Classical and classical style repertoire

- Albéniz, Mateo—Sonata in D Major

- Voříšek, Jan Václav—Rondo in G Major, op. 18, no. 1

List C: Repertoire from the romantic, 20th and 21st centuries

- Gardiner, Mary—CMC Night Sounds

- Gerou, Tom—Piece by Piece, 2 ALF 1 A Touch of Jazz

Level 8

Recommended repertoire:

List A: Baroque repertoire

- Bach, Carl Philipp Emanuel—Solfeggio in C Minor, Wq 117/2, H 220

- Galuppi, Baldassare—Sonata in D Major, op. 1, no. 4 (Adagio)

List B: Classical repertoire

- Hummel, Johann Nepomuk—Six pièces très faciles, op. 52 1 Rondo in C Major (no. 6)

- Park, Maria Hester—Sonata in F Major, op. 4, no. 1 1 1st movement

List C: Romantic repertoire

- Kalinnikov, Vasili—Chanson triste

- Wiggins, Thomas—Water in the Moonlight.

Strategies for Effective Repertoire Practice

Learning and mastering the RCM repertoire requires effective practice. Here are some strategies that can help:

- **Slow practice:** You can start by learning a new piece at a slow tempo, and that helps you ensure a solid understanding of notes and rhythm.

- **Concentrating on sections:** Break a piece into smaller sections that can make the practice more manageable and effective.

- **Practicing with separate hands:** You can start by practicing with one hand at a time. This can help focus on the specific technical challenges of each hand.

- **Increasing the tempo gradually:** Once you are comfortable with the notes and rhythm, you can start to increase the tempo gradually.

In addition, it is important to pay attention to musical details such as articulation, dynamics, and phrasing. Active listening while practicing can help you internalize these musical elements and improve your interpretation of each piece. Remember, effective practice is not only about playing the right notes but also about conveying the composer's musical intent.

One of the key points to succeed in the RCM program learning process is the choice of an appropriate repertoire for the exam that corresponds to each level. This should be selected based on the full knowledge of their compositions in order to master them technically, and also by making sure the interpretation provided is made with warmth and passion in every note to convey their true spirit.

Each piece you master will deepen your musical knowledge and also further develop your curiosity to continue exploring other works, which will lead you step by step to become an integral artist.

Playing the piano requires strength, dexterity, finger and arm strength to play the keys, as well as foot and leg strength to use the pedals. All of these constitute important degrees of skill. We will discuss these concepts in the next chapter.

Every piece learned, and every repertoire played nourishes your knowledge and lifts your spirits. Let's keep learning!

Chapter 3

Building Dexterity and Strength—A Guide to RCM Technical Studies

When we sit in front of the piano, our hands become architects. Technical studies are the bricks of our piano performance, but what is beyond the notes? How do we transform these mechanical exercises into an artistic expression that resonates in the listener's soul?

Now, imagine you are building a house. Bricks are essential for raising the walls, but they are not enough. You need mortar to join them, creating a solid structure. Similarly, technical exercises are the building blocks of our piano skills—scales, arpeggios, octave passages, and triads. But we need more than just these blocks. Creativity is the mortar that binds them, transforming technique into art.

So, use your technical studies as building blocks, but don't forget to add the cement of creativity and expression. Let your fingers dance on the keys, and you will see how the music comes to life.

In this chapter, we will explore the relevance and benefits of technical studies within the RCM program. These play an important role in the development of piano skills. They are not just routine exercises; they are also fundamental to building a solid foundation in piano technique.

The Power of Technical Studies

Technical studies can significantly benefit you when incorporated into your daily repertoire and practice exercises. Among the main benefits they provide, they improve coordination, strength, endurance, precision, and consistency when playing a piece. Each of these benefits is a foundation for progressive musical growth.

As mentioned above, coordination between hands is essential for fluid performance. Technical studies, such as scales in octaves or thirds, help to smooth transitions between notes in different hands. Constant practice of these exercises refines hand-hand coordination and facilitates the execution of complicated passages.

Technical exercises strengthen finger and hand muscles, increasing endurance. This lets musicians play longer without fatigue, which is especially valuable during concerts or recitals.

In addition, it helps you improve precision and consistency when interpreting a piece. By working on scales, arpeggios, and technical passages, musicians learn to maintain uniform articulation and precise tuning; attention to detail in each interpreted work is reflected in their general way of playing.

Exploring Different Types of Technical Studies

Scales and arpeggios are the basis for understanding the harmonic and melodic structure of music. By studying different types of scales and arpeggios, pianists acquire a deeper understanding of music theory and chord construction. As an important but extra fact, chords are the fundamental piece in the construction of a work, and in genres like jazz, musicians improvise using chords as a starting point.

Practicing them helps you strengthen and coordinate the fingers, allowing each one to move independently. In addition, the constant repetition of these patterns improves uniformity in execution. As a result, regular exercise of these technical figures helps develop muscle memory, which facilitates the interpretation of more complex musical pieces.

But what is a *scale*? It can be defined as "a group of notes that are played in sequence in ascending—major scale—or descending—minor scale—tone." In the ascending form, each note has a higher tone than the previous one, while in the descending form, each note has a lower tone than the previous one.

The main scales most used on the piano are:

- **Major scale:** The major scale is composed of eight notes, and each of these is separated from the other by a tone or semitone. This one is characterized by its cheerful and bright sound.

- **Minor scale:** The minor scale is also a sequence of notes, but it has a different character. It is based on a minor tonality and characterizes a feeling of melancholy or sadness.

- **Chromatic scale:** The chromatic scale is unique because it contains all the notes. Its distinctive feature is that there is a semitone distance between them. Imagine it as having all the colors on a musical palette.

On the other hand, *arpeggios* are "a group of notes that together form a certain chord." Among the types of arpeggios, we can highlight:

- **Triads:** These are chords formed by three notes, built from a fundamental note, a third, and a fifth. Triads are the basis of many more complex chords. There are four main types of triads: major, minor, augmented, and diminished.

- **Seventh chords:** These are chords that include a seventh—they are at a distance of seven degrees from the fundamental note. There are several types of seventh chords: dominant seventh, major seventh, minor seventh, and diminished seventh.

As a recommendation, when practicing, it is essential to take into account these three important aspects:

- **Finger patterns:** Learn different fingering patterns for scales and arpeggios. For example, the 1-2-3-1-2-3-4 pattern for major scales.

- **Articulation:** Practice with different articulations such as legato and staccato to develop control and expression. Explore different ways of playing notes, such as tied, accented, short-long, and long-short.

- **Varied tempos:** Alternate between slow and fast tempos to improve endurance and precision.

In addition, each level of the Royal Conservatory of Music presents several technical challenges by level.

The initial level focuses on posture to avoid injuries and tensions, coordination of the hands to develop better balance, and the introduction to reading notes and understanding the relationship between these and the piano keys.

Intermediate levels work on agility and speed, presenting technical challenges such as mastering major and minor scales in all keys—in addition to working on finger independence to play more complex pieces.

And advanced levels address virtuoso passages where the pieces have to be interpreted with precision and expression; also, they seek to master large jumps between notes and chords that span various octaves.

Burnam, Czerny, & Hanon's Technical Exercises

In the journey of learning the piano, technical exercises play a crucial role in developing the fundamental skills necessary for proficient playing. Three of the most renowned collections of technical exercises are by Edna Mae Burnam, Carl Czerny, and Charles-Louis Hanon. Each of these collections offers unique approaches to building finger strength, dexterity, and independence, making them invaluable resources for pianists at various levels. This section will delve into the specifics of Burnam's A Dozen A Day, Czerny's various works, and Hanon's The Virtuoso Pianist in Sixty Exercises. We will explore the structure, purpose, and appropriate levels for each set of exercises, providing a comprehensive guide to incorporating these essential tools into your practice routine.

A Dozen A Day Edna Mae Burnam's A Dozen A Day series is a beloved collection of technical exercises designed to help students develop fundamental piano skills. The exercises are structured to be short and approachable, making them ideal for incorporating into daily practice routines. This series is widely used in piano pedagogy due to its effectiveness in building technique through simple, repetitive patterns that gradually increase in complexity.

A Dozen A Day consists of several books, each tailored to different skill levels. The books are structured to provide a variety of exercises that target specific technical skills, such as finger strength, coordination, and agility. The exercises are presented in a progressive manner, making them suitable for students from beginner to intermediate levels.

The Mini Book (pink) is designed to introduce very young beginners or absolute beginners to the fundamentals of piano playing. The primary focus is on developing initial finger strength and coordination through simple and engaging exercises. These exercises help students become comfortable with basic hand positions and movements on the keyboard. The simplicity and repetitive nature of the patterns make them ideal for building muscle memory and promoting a solid foundation for future technical development. By using playful and imaginative names for the exercises, the Mini Book aims to make practice enjoyable and accessible, fostering a positive early experience with the piano.

The Preparatory Book (blue) builds upon the skills introduced in the Mini Book, gradually increasing the complexity of the exercises. It aims to enhance finger strength, agility, and coordination by introducing more advanced five-finger patterns and basic scales. The exercises in this book help students transition from very basic movements to more refined techniques, such as smooth finger crossings and basic hand independence. Additionally, the book starts to incorporate simple rhythmic patterns, including eighth notes and basic syncopation, which are essential for developing a sense of timing and rhythm. The Preparatory Book prepares students for more structured and challenging pieces by reinforcing essential technical skills in a progressive manner.

Book One (green) focuses on developing more advanced finger independence and coordination. The exercises are designed to challenge students with expanded five-finger patterns and more complex scales. This book introduces rhythmic complexities such as syncopation, which helps students develop a better sense of timing and musicality. Finger crossings and extensions are also introduced, promoting flexibility and smooth transitions across the keyboard. By working through these exercises, students build the technical accuracy and control needed to tackle more complex musical pieces. The goal is to prepare students for a broader range of repertoire by enhancing their overall technical proficiency and musical understanding.

Book Two (orange) aims to further solidify the technical foundation established in the earlier books by introducing more challenging exercises. These exercises focus on developing speed, dexterity, and control, which are crucial for intermediate-level playing. The book includes advanced finger patterns and scales, as well as more intricate rhythms and dynamic contrasts. This helps students refine their finger strength and precision, enabling them to execute faster and more complex passages with ease. The exercises are designed to promote consistent practice and technical growth, ensuring that students are well-prepared for the demands of more advanced repertoire.

Book Three (red) prepares students for advanced repertoire by focusing on exercises that require significant technical proficiency. The book introduces complex finger patterns and extended scales, challenging students to develop greater finger strength, speed, and coordination. Advanced rhythmic patterns and syncopation are also emphasized, helping students improve their timing and expressive capabilities. The exercises in Book Three are designed to enhance dynamic control and musical expression, ensuring that students can perform with both technical accuracy and artistic sensitivity. This book serves as a bridge to more advanced playing, equipping students with the skills needed to tackle challenging pieces with confidence.

Book Four (also orange) introduces more complex technical challenges, preparing students for advanced pieces. The exercises focus on developing finger independence, coordination, and technical fluency. By incorporating highly advanced finger exercises, intricate scales, and arpeggios, students are pushed to enhance their agility and control. Rapid movements and hand coordination are emphasized, ensuring that students can execute fast passages and complex rhythms with precision. The goal of Book Four is to provide rigorous technical practice that helps students transition to early advanced levels, equipping them with the necessary skills to perform more demanding repertoire.

Note: The colors and numbers of the books might be different in your region. In the UK, it is the same six books but called Mini Book, Book One: Preparatory, Book Two: Elementary, Book Three: Transitional, Book Four: Lower-Higher, and Book Five: Intermediate.

The first few books are more useful because there are less études at these levels to compete with, but for books 3 and 4 you might be better off doing études at that level instead.

Edna Mae Burnam's A Dozen A Day series is a valuable resource for developing fundamental piano skills. By systematically working through these exercises, students can build a strong technical foundation, enabling them to progress through the RCM levels with confidence and ease.

Czerny Technical Exercises and Études Carl Czerny is one of the most influential figures in piano pedagogy, known for his extensive collection of etudes and exercises designed to develop various aspects of piano technique. Czerny's works are a staple in the education of pianists, providing a bridge between basic technical exercises and the performance of more complex repertoire. He was a student of Beethoven and a teacher of Franz Liszt. He is considered to be the father of modern piano technique.

Czerny exercises are more musical than you will see in Hanon exercises, but perhaps not quite as musical as many études.

Carl Czerny's Op. 599 Practical Method for Beginners on the Pianoforte is one of the most enduring and popular collections of technical exercises for piano students. This comprehensive collection is specifically designed to introduce beginners to the fundamental techniques of piano playing, making it an invaluable resource for both students and teachers.

The Op. 599 collection is meticulously crafted to guide students through the early stages of piano education. It focuses on basic finger exercises, simple pieces, and essential musical concepts, all presented in a progressive order of difficulty. The method is structured to build a strong technical foundation, ensuring that students develop the necessary skills to advance confidently.

The initial exercises in Op. 599 emphasize finger strength and independence. These exercises are designed to ensure that students develop proper hand positioning and finger movement from the very beginning. The collection includes a variety of short, simple pieces that help students apply the techniques they learn in the exercises. These pieces are not only instructive but also musically engaging, making practice more enjoyable. The exercises and pieces in Op. 599 are organized in a sequence that gradually increases in difficulty. This progressive approach allows students to build their skills step-by-step, without becoming overwhelmed. The method starts at a beginner level and advances to approximately RCM Level 4. Alongside technical exercises, Czerny's method introduces essential musical concepts such as dynamics, articulation, and phrasing. This holistic approach ensures that students not only develop technical proficiency but also musical expressiveness.

Czerny's Op. 599 Practical Method for Beginners on the Pianoforte remains a cornerstone of piano education, valued for its structured approach to developing essential piano skills. Whether used under the guidance of a teacher or as part of a self-directed study, this collection provides a solid foundation for aspiring pianists, paving the way for more advanced studies and a lifelong enjoyment of music.

In addition to his well-known Op. 599 Practical Method for Beginners on the Pianoforte, Carl Czerny composed several other collections of exercises designed to support the early stages of piano education. These works include Op. 823 The Little Pianist, Op. 777 24 Exercises for the Five Fingers, and Op. 261 125 Exercises for Passage Playing. Each of these collections focuses on specific technical aspects of piano playing and is structured to progressively build the skills necessary for more advanced repertoire.

The Little Pianist is designed to introduce young students to piano playing through a series of short, engaging pieces and exercises. This collection aims to develop basic technical skills while keeping the learning process enjoyable and motivating for young learners.

The Op. 777 24 Exercises for the Five Fingers collection focuses specifically on developing finger strength, independence, and dexterity. These exercises are designed to ensure that each finger, particularly the weaker fourth and fifth fingers, is developed equally.

125 Exercises for Passage Playing is designed to help students develop smooth, even passage work, which is essential for playing scales, arpeggios, and other technical runs. This collection targets the fluidity and accuracy of finger movements across various passages.

After selectively working through Op. 599 Practical Method for Beginners on the Pianoforte, students may wish to progress to Czerny's works designed for intermediate and advanced levels. These collections build on the foundation established by Op. 599, introducing more complex exercises that target specific technical skills necessary for advanced piano playing.

Op. 849 30 Études (Studies of Mechanism) is designed to prepare students for more demanding technical exercises, such as those found in Op. 299 The School of Velocity. This collection focuses on developing the mechanisms of piano playing, including finger strength, independence, and coordination. The études cover various technical challenges, such as finger dexterity, hand coordination, and precision in playing scales and arpeggios. Each study targets a specific aspect of technique, gradually increasing in difficulty. By working through these études, students build a solid technical foundation, enhancing their readiness for the rapid and intricate passages encountered in more advanced studies.

Op. 299 The School of Velocity is designed to enhance finger speed, precision, and agility. It is suitable for students at grades 5-8 (RCM levels) and focuses on developing the skills needed for playing rapid note passages, scales, and arpeggios with accuracy and evenness. The études here are characterized by their emphasis on rapid, flowing finger movements. These exercises help students develop the ability to play quickly and smoothly, maintaining clarity and control. Regular practice of these études improves overall finger dexterity and speed, making it easier to execute fast passages in more complex pieces.

Op. 139 100 Progressive Studies provides a comprehensive set of intermediate studies that are particularly useful for younger students or those with smaller hands, as these exercises do not include octaves. The studies progress in difficulty, starting with simpler exercises and gradually introducing more challenging technical elements. They cover a range of skills, including articulation, finger strength, and rhythmic precision. These progressive studies help students develop a well-rounded technical foundation without the strain of playing octaves, making them ideal for building technique in a gradual and manageable way.

Op. 636 Preliminary School of Finger Dexterity serves as a preparatory collection for Czerny's more advanced technical studies, such as Op. 740 The Art of Finger Dexterity. It focuses on developing the initial stages of finger agility and control. The exercises in this collection emphasize finger independence, control, and the ability to execute rapid, precise movements. They prepare students for the more complex fingerings and technical challenges found in advanced études. Completing Op. 636 equips students with the necessary technical foundation to tackle the more demanding exercises in Op. 740, ensuring a smoother transition to advanced studies.

Op. 740 The Art of Finger Dexterity is aimed at developing advanced technical skills, including complex fingerings, rapid passages, and intricate hand coordination. It is designed for students at the early advanced level and beyond (RCM levels 8-10). The études here are highly challenging, requiring precise finger control, agility, and the ability to navigate complex musical textures. These exercises cover a broad range of technical aspects, from fast scale passages to intricate fingerings. Regular practice of these études significantly enhances technical proficiency, preparing students for the most demanding piano repertoire. The skills developed through these exercises are essential for achieving technical mastery and expressive performance in advanced pieces.

Czerny's works are invaluable resources for pianists aiming to develop their technique systematically. By incorporating these studies into their practice, students can build a solid technical foundation, enabling them to perform more advanced repertoire with ease and confidence.

Hanon Charles-Louis Hanon's The Virtuoso Pianist in Sixty Exercises is a staple in piano pedagogy, renowned for its effectiveness in developing finger strength, independence, and dexterity. These exercises are designed to address various technical challenges and are used by pianists at different stages of their development.

Hanon's collection is divided into three parts, each progressively increasing in difficulty. The exercises focus on repetitive finger patterns that target specific technical skills, making them suitable for daily practice routines.

The first part of Hanon's exercises (exercises 1-20) is aimed at building basic finger strength and agility. These exercises are relatively simple and repetitive, making them ideal for beginners who are developing their fundamental piano skills. These are appropriate from Preparatory A to RCM Level 4.

The second part (exercises 21-43) builds on the foundation laid in the first part, introducing more complex patterns and increasing the speed and range of motion. These exercises are designed to further enhance finger independence and strength. These are appropriate from RCM Levels 4-6.

The final part of Hanon's exercises (exercises 44-60) is geared toward advanced students, featuring highly challenging patterns that require significant technical proficiency. These exercises are intended to prepare pianists for the demands of advanced repertoire. These are appropriate from RCM Levels 6-8.

Deciding Whether to Add These Exercises to Your Program

After exploring the distinct benefits and structures of the technical exercises by Burnam, Czerny, and Hanon, the question arises: should these exercises be added to your piano practice program? The answer largely depends on your individual goals, current skill level, and specific technical needs.

For Beginners and Early Learners: Burnam's A Dozen A Day series is highly recommended. Its progressive and engaging exercises are ideal for building foundational skills in a fun and approachable way. These exercises can seamlessly integrate into daily practice routines, making technical development enjoyable and less monotonous.

For Intermediate Students: Czerny's studies, such as The School of Velocity, Op. 299, offer excellent opportunities to enhance finger speed, precision, and coordination. Incorporating these exercises can help intermediate students tackle more complex repertoire with greater confidence and technical proficiency.

For Advanced Pianists: Hanon's The Virtuoso Pianist in Sixty Exercises and Czerny's The Art of Finger Dexterity, Op. 740, provide rigorous technical challenges that are essential for advanced pianists. These exercises focus on building superior finger independence, strength, and agility, which are crucial for performing advanced pieces with accuracy and expression.

For a well-rounded technical development, combining exercises from all three collections can be highly beneficial. This approach ensures that pianists develop a broad range of skills, from basic coordination and strength to advanced dexterity and speed.

While the benefits of technical exercises are substantial, there are also potential downsides to consider:

Technical exercises, by their nature, are repetitive. While repetition is key to developing muscle memory and technical proficiency, it can also become monotonous. This repetitiveness can lead to boredom, reducing motivation and engagement in practice. There are also many similar exercises dealing with the same technique that can become repetitive if you do all the exercises.

Without proper technique and mindful practice, the repetitive nature of these exercises can lead to strain or injury. It's crucial to practice with correct posture, hand position, and relaxation to avoid overuse injuries. Regular breaks and varied practice routines can also help mitigate this risk. Ignore the recommendation in Hanon to lift fingers high while holding the forearm and wrist tense.

Technical exercises often focus on mechanical aspects of playing, which can seem unmusical compared to practicing actual pieces. This can lead to a disconnect between technical practice and musical expression if not balanced properly. It's important to integrate musical pieces alongside technical exercises to maintain a holistic approach to learning.

Relying too heavily on technical exercises can sometimes result in an overemphasis on technique at the expense of musicality and expression. Pianists should strive to balance technical practice with repertoire that encourages musical interpretation and creativity.

Ultimately, adding Burnam, Czerny, and Hanon's exercises to your program can significantly enhance your technical abilities, leading to more confident and expressive performances. Regular, focused practice of these exercises will help you build a solid technical foundation, enabling you to tackle a diverse repertoire with greater ease and musicality.

Conquering Technical Challenges: Effective Practice Strategies

The first step to overcoming technical challenges when playing the piano is to set SMART goals—specific, measurable, achievable, relevant, and time-bound. By setting such goals for your technical practice, you can focus on specific aspects that you want to improve; as a result, it will help you set realistic and achievable goals for your technical studies.

Encourage yourself to set your SMART goals following these examples as a recommendation:

- **Specific:** Goals should be clear and precise. For example, instead of saying, "I want to improve my piano technique," a specific goal could be, "I want to improve my ability to play chromatic scales on the piano."

- **Measurable:** You should be able to measure your progress toward the goal. For example, you could decide to practice chromatic scales for 15 minutes a day and then gradually increase this time as you feel more comfortable.

- **Achievable:** Goals should be realistic and achievable. If you are a beginner, it would not be realistic to set a goal of playing a piece of Chopin perfectly in a week. A more achievable goal could be to learn to play a chromatic scale at a moderate tempo without errors.

- **Relevant:** If your overall goal is to improve your piano technique, then practicing chromatic scales is pertinent, as these are fundamental to multiple pieces of music.

- **Time-bound:** You should set a deadline to achieve your goal. This will help you maintain motivation and track your progress. For example, you could set the goal of being able to play a major or minor scale at a moderate tempo without errors in a month.

One of the keys to mastering technical challenges is having slow and deliberate practice. This means that you should take your time without rushing. An effective strategy is to divide difficult passages into smaller sections and practice gradually increasing the tempo as you improve precision and control. Remember, patience is a virtue when it comes to learning to play the piano.

Finally, it is important to seek precision and consistency in your technical practice. This means you should strive to play and feel each note while maintaining a constant rhythm. Repeat complicated sections until you can play them smoothly before moving on, and don't forget to use a metronome, as it can be of great help in developing a constant tempo and excellent rhythmic precision.

Overcoming Common Technical Hurdles

Playing the piano is an exciting journey filled with rewards and challenges. One of the most common challenges piano students face is technical obstacles. These can range from uneven finger strength to tension and incorrect hand position.

Uneven finger strength can make some notes sound louder than others, which can affect the melody of the music. To overcome this challenge, it is helpful to practice scales and arpeggios, as these exercises help develop finger strength and independence.

Tension is another common technical obstacle. Playing the piano with tension can lead to injuries and can also affect the sound quality. An effective way to overcome tension is to ensure the posture when playing is correct. This includes keeping the back straight, the shoulders relaxed, and the wrists flexible.

Incorrect hand position can also cause technical problems. The hands should be in a natural and relaxed position as if you were holding a small ball. Practicing this position helps improve technique and prevent injuries.

In addition to these tips, it is important to remember that each student is unique and faces specific technical challenges. Therefore, seeking guidance from a qualified teacher from the Royal Conservatory of Music is highly recommended, as they can provide personalized solutions and effective practice strategies to overcome any technical difficulty.

In summary, overcoming technical obstacles in piano learning requires focused practice, awareness of posture and hand position, and seeking guidance from an experienced teacher. With patience and dedication, these challenges can be overcome, allowing students to fully enjoy the beautiful art of playing the piano.

In this chapter, we have explored the importance and effective practice of RCM technical studies. We have seen how these studies can seem challenging at first, but they are fundamental to our development as pianists.

The journey of technical development is a continuous path. Each technique, each scale, and each arpeggio we practice has a positive impact on our overall piano playing. It helps us better understand music, interpret it more accurately, and express ourselves with greater freedom.

In the next chapter, we now shift our focus to a fundamental aspect of piano learning: the art of études. There, we will dive into the significance of them in developing technical skills, musicality, and expressive playing. Through a comprehensive exploration of various types of études, practice strategies, and integration into performance, we aim to enhance our overall musical proficiency and deepen our understanding of the piano repertoire.

Chapter 4

Études—Enhancing Technical Proficiency and Musicality with the RCM Method

Before we begin this chapter, imagine a young pianist eagerly flipping through a stack of sheet music. Among the sonatas and concertos, one piece stands out: a collection of études by a renowned composer. Intrigued, the pianist begins to dive into these seemingly simple yet deceptively complex pieces.

At first, each étude presents a unique challenge—a flurry of rapid notes testing finger agility, a cascade of arpeggios demanding precision, or a lyrical melody requiring delicate phrasing. Frustration and determination intermingle as the pianist grapples with technical hurdles and seeks to unlock the music's deeper meaning.

Yet, with each focused practice session, something occurs. The pianist's fingers grow stronger and more nimble, effortlessly gliding across the keys. Musical phrases once disjointed now flow seamlessly, imbued with emotion and artistry. What began as a study in technique evolves into a journey of musical discovery and self-expression.

This story reflects the essence of études—a blend of technical study and musical exploration that lies at the heart of every pianist's journey. In this chapter, you'll learn about the significance of études, explore their diverse forms and challenges, and understand strategies to turn these musical studies into tools for enhancing your overall musical proficiency.

Introduction to Études

Études is a French word meaning 'study' and they are pieces designed to develop specific technical skills while also offering musical challenges. In this chapter, we'll delve into the significance of études in your piano journey, explore various types, and discuss strategies for practicing them effectively to enhance your overall musical proficiency.

*É*tudes are like musical workouts, targeting different aspects of piano playing, such as finger agility, hand coordination, strength, endurance, and expressive playing. They not only refine your technical abilities but also deepen your understanding of musical interpretation and style.

Études hold an important place in the life of every pianist, offering a structured path toward developing not just technical prowess but also musicality and expressive playing. Their importance lies in the multifaceted benefits they bring to a pianist's development.

Firstly, études are invaluable for honing technical skills. These pieces are crafted to address specific technical challenges, whether mastering rapid finger work, intricate hand coordination, or navigating complex scale and arpeggio patterns. Through dedicated practice of études, pianists develop dexterity, precision, and control in their fingers, laying a solid foundation for tackling more demanding repertoire with confidence and ease.

Secondly, despite their technical focus, études are also musical compositions, often containing melodic lines, harmonic progressions, and expressive markings. This dual nature allows pianists to integrate technical proficiency with musical expression.

Lastly, études contribute significantly to the development of expressive playing. As pianists dive into each étude, they discover opportunities to express a wide range of emotions and musical ideas. Through careful interpretation and attention to detail, pianists transform these technical exercises into artistic expressions, moods, and feelings through their playing. This blend of technical mastery and artistic sensitivity is essential for captivating performances that resonate with audiences.

Different Types of Études and Their Role in the RCM Curriculum

In the Royal Conservatory of Music curriculum, études play a vital role in shaping pianists' technical abilities, musical understanding, and stylistic versatility across levels 1–8. Let's explore the different types of études.

Technical Études

Technical études focus primarily on developing specific technical skills essential for piano playing. In the RCM curriculum, technical études are carefully selected to align with the technical requirements of each level. For example, early levels may include études focusing on basic finger patterns and hand coordination, while advanced levels incorporate complex passages, double-note techniques, and virtuosic elements. Technical études are instrumental in building a solid technical foundation, enabling pianists to navigate challenging repertoire with confidence and precision.

Musical Études

Musical études go beyond technical exercises; they are musical compositions designed to develop interpretive and expressive skills. In the RCM curriculum, musical études are selected to expose students to a variety of musical styles and genres. For instance, students may encounter Baroque-style études focusing on clarity and ornamentation, Romantic-era études emphasizing lyricism and emotion, or Contemporary études exploring innovative techniques and soundscapes. Musical études help pianists create an understanding of musical interpretation, encouraging them to convey emotions, moods, and storytelling through their playing.

Stylistic Études

Stylistic études dive into specific musical styles, periods, or composers, allowing pianists to immerse themselves in stylistic authenticity and historical context. These études require not only technical proficiency but also a deep understanding of the characteristics, nuances, and performance practices associated with each style. In the RCM curriculum, stylistic études are integrated to broaden students' repertoire knowledge and stylistic awareness. For example, students may explore Baroque dance suites, classical sonata forms, romantic character pieces, or impressionistic tone poems through stylistic études. By engaging with a diverse range of styles, pianists develop a versatile and well-rounded approach to interpreting different musical genres.

In the RCM curriculum, the inclusion of various types of études serves multiple purposes:

- Technical mastery: Technical études strengthen pianists' technical foundations, enabling them to execute challenging passages with accuracy and control.

- Expressive playing: Musical études foster expressive and interpretive skills, encouraging pianists to imbue their playing with emotion, phrasing, and musicality.

- Stylistic versatility: Stylistic études expose pianists to a wide range of musical styles and genres, enhancing their stylistic awareness and performance adaptability.

- Artistic development: Collectively, études contribute to pianists' artistic development, shaping them into well-rounded musicians capable of tackling diverse repertoire with confidence and artistry.

Benefits of Practicing Études

Practicing études offers a plethora of benefits that contribute to a pianist's overall development and mastery of the instrument. These include:

Improved Finger Dexterity, Hand Coordination, and Agility

Études are designed to challenge and refine your finger dexterity, hand coordination, and agility. Through repetitive and focused practice of technical passages, scales, arpeggios, and patterns, you train your fingers to move swiftly and accurately across the keyboard. This improves not only your physical control but also your ability to execute complex passages with fluidity and precision. Over time, you'll notice increased ease and fluency in playing demanding pieces, thanks to the foundational skills developed through practicing études.

Enhanced Musical Interpretation, Phrasing, and Dynamics

While technical proficiency is crucial, musicality is what brings music to life. Études offer opportunities to enhance your musical interpretation, phrasing, and dynamics. Each étude presents a unique musical challenge, whether it's shaping a melodic line, crafting nuanced dynamics, or creating expressive phrasing.

Development of Specific Technical Skills through Musical Context

One of the remarkable aspects of études is their ability to develop specific technical skills within a musical context. Rather than isolated exercises, études integrate technical challenges seamlessly into musical compositions. For example, études focusing on scales help you master scale patterns and fingerings while exploring melodic variations and harmonic progressions. Similarly, études centered on arpeggios strengthen your ability to navigate chordal passages with ease and musicality. This integration of technical skills within musical contexts not only makes practicing more enjoyable but also facilitates a deeper understanding of how technical elements contribute to overall musical expression.

In addition to these primary benefits, practicing études offers many other advantages:

- Strengthening of weak areas: Études allow you to target and strengthen specific technical areas that may be challenging or underdeveloped since these provide focused exercises to address and overcome these weaknesses.

- Building confidence: Mastering études instills a sense of accomplishment and confidence in your playing. As you conquer technical challenges and refine your musical interpretation, you gain confidence in tackling a more complex repertoire with assurance and poise.

- Expanding repertoire: Many études are miniature compositions that showcase various styles, techniques, and musical concepts. By practicing a diverse range of études, you expand your musical vocabulary and repertoire knowledge, enriching your playing and interpretation skills across different genres and periods.

- Long-term progress: Consistent practice of études contributes to long-term progress and growth as a pianist. The skills and insights gained from practicing études carry over into your performance of repertoire, allowing you to approach pieces with greater technical proficiency, musicality, and artistry.

Selection of Études

Selecting the right études is crucial for effective and targeted practice that aligns with the pianist's skill level and developmental needs. The criteria include:

- Technical difficulty: Consider the technical demands of the études, such as hand coordination, speed, and accuracy. Choose études that provide appropriate challenges without being overwhelmingly difficult for the current skill level.

- Musicality: Look for études that offer musical challenges in addition to technical exercises. These études should encourage musical interpretation, phrasing, dynamics, and expression, enhancing your musicality alongside technical proficiency.

- Progression: Select études that align with your progression and development. Études should gradually increase in difficulty, allowing for a progressive and systematic approach to skill improvement.

- Relevance to repertoire: Consider the musical style, genre, and techniques featured in your current repertoire. Choose études that complement and reinforce the skills needed for performing repertoire pieces at the respective level.

- Interest and engagement: Prioritize études that resonate with your musical interests and goals. Engaging with music that inspires and motivates promotes focused and effective practice.

Recommended Études for RCM Levels

RCM Level 1   Étude: Czerny—the School of Velocity, Op. 299, No. 1

- Technical challenges: Legato phrasing, basic hand coordination, dynamic contrasts.

- Musical challenges: Expressive shaping of simple melodies and building finger strength.

RCM Level 2   Étude: Burgmüller—25 Easy and Progressive Studies, Op. 100, No. 2 *Arabesque*

- Technical challenges: Articulation control, coordination between hands, moderate tempo.

- Musical challenges: Graceful phrasing, balance between melody and accompaniment.

RCM Level 3   Étude: Czerny—Practical Method for Beginners on the Pianoforte, Op. 599, No. 11

- Technical challenges: Scale passages, legato playing, dynamic control.

- Musical challenges: Developing fluency in scale patterns and exploring dynamics for musical expression.

RCM Level 4   Étude: Heller—25 Melodious Studies, Op. 45, No. 2

- Technical challenges: Double-note passages, hand independence, agility in finger work.

- Musical challenges: Shaping melodic lines with clarity and navigating chromatic passages.

RCM Level 5   Étude: Czerny—School of Velocity, Op. 299, No. 9

- Technical challenges: Rapid scale runs, dynamic contrasts, staccato articulation.

- Musical challenges: Achieving evenness and control in fast passages and interpreting dynamic markings.

RCM Level 6   Étude: Burgmüller—25 Progressive Studies, Op. 100, No. 13 *Ballade*

- Technical challenges: Broken chords, arpeggios, legato and staccato combination.

- Musical challenges: Expressive phrasing, balance between chordal and melodic elements.

RCM Level 7   Étude: Chopin—Étude in C Major, Op. 10, No. 1 *Waterfall*

- Technical challenges: Rapid arpeggios, hand coordination, dynamic control.

- Musical challenges: Sustaining fluidity and clarity in arpeggio patterns and exploring nuances in dynamics and touch.

RCM Level 8   Étude: Liszt—Transcendental Étude No. 1 *Preludio*

- Technical challenges: Virtuosic passages, octaves, rapid chromatic runs.

- Musical challenges: Balancing technical demands with musical expression and conveying dramatic intensity and brilliance.

Considerations in a Practice Routine

Balancing technical exercises, repertoire, and étude practice is essential for maintaining a well-rounded and effective practice routine in piano learning. Here are some considerations to help you achieve a harmonious balance:

Identify Priorities

Begin by identifying your current priorities and goals. Determine whether your focus is on building technical proficiency, mastering repertoire pieces, or refining specific musical skills. This clarity will guide how you allocate time and resources in your practice routine.

Allocate Time Wisely

Divide your practice session into dedicated segments for technical exercises, repertoire practice, and étude work. Allocate time based on your priorities and the specific areas that require attention. For example, if technical skills need improvement, allocate more time to technical exercises and études.

Integrate Technical and Musical Elements

Merge technical exercises with musical elements to create a seamless practice experience. Incorporate scales, arpeggios, and finger exercises within musical contexts, such as études or repertoire pieces. This integration not only enhances technical skills but also reinforces their application in real musical scenarios.

Practice Efficiency

Practice efficiently by focusing on targeted goals and using effective practice strategies. Break down challenging passages into smaller segments, use metronome practice for tempo control, and employ practice techniques such as slow practice, hands-separate practice, and varied articulation to enhance learning and retention.

Rotate Repertoire Pieces

Rotate repertoire pieces in your practice routine to maintain freshness and avoid burnout. Work on a mix of pieces at different levels of difficulty, genres, and styles. This variety keeps your practice engaging and allows for continuous progress across a diverse repertoire.

Monitor Progress

Regularly assess your progress and adjust your practice routine as needed. Keep track of technical improvements, musical interpretations, and performance skills. Seek feedback from teachers or mentors to gain valuable insights and guidance for refining your practice approach.

Maintain Consistency

Consistency is key to effective practice. Establish a regular practice schedule that suits your lifestyle and commitments. Aim for daily practice sessions, even if they are shorter in duration, to maintain momentum and continuity in your learning journey.

Practice Strategies of Études

Practicing études effectively is a blend of strategic approaches, focused techniques, and systematic methods that contribute to a pianist's overall growth and proficiency.

Warm-up Exercises for Études

Finger Exercises   Start your practice session with fundamental finger exercises to enhance dexterity, control, and agility. Scales, arpeggios, and chromatic exercises are excellent warm-ups that target finger independence, evenness, and coordination between hands. Begin at a slow tempo, focusing on clarity and accuracy, then gradually increase the speed as your fingers warm up. Pay attention to fingerings, hand positioning, and a relaxed yet controlled touch to ensure smooth execution of technical passages in études.

Hand Coordination   Include exercises that promote hand coordination and synchronization. Parallel motion scales and arpeggios, contrary motion scales, and octave exercises are beneficial for improving hand independence and coordination. Pay attention to maintaining a consistent sound quality and balanced touch between hands. Focus on achieving evenness and clarity in both hands, especially in passages that require rapid movement or complex fingerings.

Technical Patterns   Practice technical patterns relevant to the étude you'll be working on. This could include rapid passages, intervallic jumps, chord progressions, or specific fingerings. By familiarizing yourself with these technical elements during warm-up, you prepare your fingers and mind for the challenges ahead in the étude. Focus on executing technical patterns with precision, control, and musicality, paying attention to dynamics, articulation, and phrasing.

Breaking Down Études Into Manageable Sections

Phrasing and Musical Sections   Identify distinct phrases and musical sections within the étude. Work on each phrase individually, focusing on musical shaping, dynamics, articulation, and expression. Practice with a singing tone, paying attention to the natural flow and contour of the music. Experiment with different phrasing options, dynamics, and expressive techniques to create a compelling and nuanced performance.

Technical Passages   Isolate technical passages that present challenges, such as rapid scales, arpeggios, or intricate fingerings. Practice these passages slowly and methodically, focusing on precision, clarity, and evenness. Use varied articulations—legato, staccato, etc.— to develop versatility in your playing and ensure smooth transitions between notes. Break down complex passages into smaller segments and practice them in isolation before integrating them back into the full context of the étude.

Hands-Separate Practice   Dedicate time to practicing each hand separately to address technical issues, fingering challenges, and coordination between hands. This focused approach allows you to concentrate on specific hand movements, fingerings, and articulations without the complexity of playing hands together initially. Once each hand feels comfortable, gradually combine them for a seamless performance. Use hands-separate practice to refine fingerings, hand positions, and coordination, ensuring clarity and accuracy in both hands.

Strategies for Addressing Technical Challenges

Slow Practice   Begin practicing challenging passages at a slow tempo to ensure accuracy, control, and understanding of the musical nuances. Focus on correct fingerings, hand positioning, and rhythmic accuracy. As you gain confidence and mastery, gradually increase the tempo while maintaining clarity and precision. Slow practice allows you to focus on details, identify areas of improvement, and build muscle memory for complex passages.

Metronome Practice Use a metronome to practice rhythmic accuracy, tempo control, and consistency. Start at a comfortable tempo and gradually increase it as you become more proficient. The metronome helps develop a steady sense of timing, improves rhythmic precision, and aids in mastering difficult passages at varying tempos. Use it to work on specific technical challenges, such as evenness in scale runs, coordination between hands, and maintaining a steady pulse.

Focused Repetition Focus on repeated practice of difficult sections, paying attention to details such as dynamics, articulation, phrasing, and expression. Use varied dynamics and articulations to explore different musical interpretations. Repetition with a purposeful focus on improvement leads to mastery and confidence in tackling technical challenges. Break down challenging passages into smaller segments and practice them repeatedly, gradually increasing speed and complexity as you improve.

Common Challenges and Solutions

Pianists often encounter common challenges that can hinder progress and motivation. Understanding these challenges and implementing effective solutions is crucial for a successful étude practice. Let's explore some of these:

Dealing With Difficult Passages, Fingerings, and Hand Positions

Identify Problematic Areas Start by identifying specific passages, fingerings, or hand positions within the étude that pose challenges. Break down the piece into smaller sections and pinpoint areas that require focused attention and practice.

Practice Slowly and Methodically Practice difficult passages at a slow tempo, focusing on accuracy, fingerings, and hand positions. Remember to use a metronome to maintain a steady pace and gradually increase the tempo as you gain control and confidence.

Utilize Practice Techniques Employ practice techniques such as hands-separate practice, rhythmic variations, and incremental learning. Practice each hand separately to address technical issues and coordination. Use rhythmic variations (e.g., dotted rhythms, triplets) to improve rhythmic accuracy and fluency.

Experiment With Fingerings Explore alternative fingerings for challenging passages to find the most efficient and comfortable approach. Consult fingering suggestions in the score, but also trust your own judgment and adapt fingerings based on your hand size and comfort.

Overcoming Mental Barriers and Developing a Positive Mindset

Set Realistic Expectations Set achievable goals and realistic expectations for your practice sessions. Break down long-term goals into smaller milestones and celebrate progress along the way. Avoid comparing yourself to others and focus on your own growth and improvement.

Embrace Challenges as Opportunities   View challenges in étude practice as opportunities for growth and learning. Embrace the process of overcoming difficulties, as it leads to improved skills, resilience, and musical development. Adopt a growth mindset that values effort, persistence, and continuous improvement.

Manage Performance Anxiety   Develop strategies to manage performance anxiety and nerves when practicing études. Practice relaxation techniques such as deep breathing. Besides, gradually expose yourself to performance situations, such as mock auditions or recordings, to build confidence and resilience.

Seeking Guidance from Teachers, Recordings, and Resources

Consult Your Teacher   Seek guidance and feedback from your piano teacher or mentor. They can provide valuable insights, practice tips, and technical advice tailored to your specific needs. Schedule regular lessons to receive ongoing support and direction in your étude practice.

Study Recordings and Performances   Listen to recordings of professional pianists performing études to gain inspiration, musical ideas, and interpretive insights. Study different interpretations and approaches to the same piece to broaden your musical perspective and understanding.

Attend Workshops and Masterclasses   Participate in workshops, masterclasses, and seminars focused on étude practice and performance. Attend live performances and observe experienced pianists in action to learn from their techniques, musicality, and stage presence.

Integration of Études Into Performance

Incorporating études into performance is a great aspect of a pianist's development, showcasing technical prowess, musicality, and artistic interpretation. Now, let's explore strategies for integrating études into recitals, exams, and performances, maintaining consistency and accuracy under pressure, and balancing technical precision with artistic expression for a compelling musical presentation.

Selection of Études

Remember to choose études that complement your repertoire and showcase your technical abilities and musicality. Consider the theme, mood, and style of the performance to select études that align with the overall program. Balance technical challenges with musicality and variety to create a well-rounded performance.

Program Planning

Integrate études strategically into your performance program. Consider the flow and pacing of the program, placing études strategically between larger works to provide contrast and highlight technical proficiency. Use études as musical interludes or transitions to enhance the overall narrative of the performance.

Contextualizing Études

Provide context for the audience by introducing each étude with brief background information, composer insights, and technical challenges. Share anecdotes, historical context, or musical analysis to engage the audience and enhance their appreciation of the étude's significance within the performance.

Strategies for Maintaining Consistency and Accuracy

Mock Performances   Simulate performance conditions through mock performances, recitals, or practice exams. Invite friends, family, or fellow musicians to listen and provide feedback. Practice performing under pressure to build confidence, identify areas for improvement, and refine your performance approach.

Mental Preparation   Develop mental preparation strategies to manage performance anxiety and nerves. Practice visualization techniques, positive self-talk, and relaxation exercises to stay focused, calm, and confident during the performance.

Balancing Technical Precision with Artistic Interpretation

Musical Understanding   Study the composer's intentions, historical background, and stylistic elements to inform your interpretation. Focus on musical phrasing, dynamics, articulation, and expressive nuances to convey the emotional depth of the music.

Technical Mastery   Achieve technical mastery through diligent practice and attention to detail. Focus on accuracy, clarity, and control in executing technical passages, fingerings, and hand positions. Use practice techniques such as slow practice, hands-separate practice, and rhythmic variations to refine technical skills.

Artistic Expression   Experiment with dynamic contrasts, tempo fluctuations, rubato, and expressive nuances to convey musicality and depth. Balance technical precision with emotional storytelling to create a compelling and engaging performance.

If you follow these strategies, you can create impactful and memorable musical presentations that showcase their technical proficiency, musicality, and expressive depth. Accept the opportunity to share the beauty and complexity of études with audiences, leaving a lasting impression through compelling and engaging performances.

So, you see, études play an important role in the piano learning journey, serving as invaluable tools for developing technical proficiency, musicality, and expressive depth. Throughout this chapter, we have explored the significance of études in piano learning within the context of the RCM method, highlighting their multifaceted benefits and practical applications across different skill levels.

These offer a structured and systematic approach to mastering various technical and musical challenges encountered in the piano repertoire. They provide opportunities for focused practice, skill development, and musical exploration, ultimately enhancing the overall musical proficiency of pianists.

The Royal Conservatory of Music (RCM) method integrates études into its curriculum to create well-rounded musicianship and technical excellence. From the foundational levels to advanced stages, études are carefully selected to address specific technical skills, musical concepts, and stylistic elements relevant to each level of piano study.

We encourage you to continue your exploration and mastery of études as an ongoing part of your musical development. Accept the challenges and rewards of étude practice, view each étude as an opportunity for growth and learning, and strive for continuous improvement in technical precision, musicality, and expressive playing.

In the next chapter, we will dive into the realm of developing musical literacy and ear training. This chapter will explore essential concepts in music theory, ear training, and musical analysis, providing a comprehensive foundation for understanding music notation, harmony, rhythm, and musical structure. Stay tuned for insights, strategies, and practical exercises to enhance your musical literacy and deepen your musical understanding. May your love for music, dedication to learning, and commitment to artistic expression guide you toward greater musical heights.

Chapter 5

Beyond the Notes—Developing Musical Literacy Through RCM Theory & Ear Training

Have you ever felt that, despite playing the notes correctly, the music seems to escape your comprehension? As if you were reading words without understanding their meaning? If so, this chapter is made for you.

Music is a language, and like any language, it requires some literacy to be understood in depth. In this chapter, we will explore the RCM's approach to music literacy, a method that will not only teach you to *read* music but also *understand* it.

Through music theory and ear training, you will learn to appreciate the subtleties and nuances that make a piece of music come alive. This knowledge will allow you to play with greater confidence and expressiveness, transforming you from a simple note player to a true pianist.

Get ready to embark on a journey that will change the way you see, hear, and, most importantly, feel music. Let's get started!

Importance of Music Theory

Music theory is the study of the practices and possibilities of music. It is the framework that allows musicians to understand the structure and components of music, including harmony, melody, rhythm, and form. By learning music theory, you will gain insights into how pieces are constructed, which will enhance your interpretive skills and deepen your appreciation of the music you play

Notation: Understanding the symbols and markings used to represent music on the page.

Rhythm: Learning about time signatures, note values, and how to keep a steady beat.

Harmony: Exploring chords, progressions, and the relationship between different notes.

Melody: Understanding how sequences of notes create memorable and expressive tunes.

Form: Recognizing the structure of a piece, such as binary, ternary, and sonata forms.

Dynamics and Articulation: Learning how to interpret and execute dynamic markings and articulation symbols to bring expressiveness to your playing.

The Power of Music Theory

Music theory can be seen as a rigid and boring set of rules, but in reality, it is a powerful tool that opens up a world of musical understanding and appreciation. Far from being a mere collection of abstract principles, music theory is the language of music, with its own alphabet, grammar, and syntax. The basic components of music, such as notes, chords, scales, and rhythms, are like the letters, words, and phrases of this language. Understanding these elements is essential to reading, performing, and creating music.

Notes are the individual sounds that form the basic building blocks of music. When combined in certain ways, they create chords, which are akin to musical words.. Chords are combinations of notes that create harmony. Chords provide the harmonic foundation of music, giving it depth and color. Scales are collections of notes arranged in ascending or descending order. Scales are like grammatical rules that tell us which notes work well together. Rhythm is the pulse or beat of the music. Rhythm gives music its sense of time and movement, creating patterns that make music dynamic and engaging.

As you progress through the Royal Conservatory of Music (RCM) levels, music theory becomes increasingly complex. Initially, you will learn the basics, such as how to read sheet music and understand musical cues. As you advance, you will delve into harmony, counterpoint, and musical forms. These concepts allow you to understand how music is structured and how different elements interact with each other.

Music theory is not just about analysis and understanding; it is also a creative tool. By understanding theory, you can experiment with different scales, chords, and rhythms to create your own music. This knowledge enables you to explore new ideas and express yourself in ways that would not be possible without a theoretical foundation.

Additionally, a solid grasp of music theory improves your ability to perform and appreciate music. By understanding the underlying structure of a piece, you can play it with greater expressiveness and depth. This deeper comprehension transforms your playing from mere note reproduction to a more nuanced and emotional performance.

To fully understand music theory, it is vital to comprehend musical notation—the graphic language used to represent songs or pieces of music. Musical notation allows artists to interpret, read, and write music. The key elements of musical notation are:

- **Staff:** It is a set of five lines and four spaces where notes and rests are written. Each line and space represents a different note.

- **Clef:** A symbol placed at the beginning of the staff to indicate the pitch of the notes. The most common are the treble clef and bass clef.

- **Accidentals:** A set of accidentals—sharps or flats—placed at the beginning of the staff to indicate the key of the piece of music.

- **Notes:** Symbols that represent musical sounds.

- **Rests:** These are the signs that represent the absence of sound. Like notes, rests have different durations.

- **Intervals:** The distance between two notes. Intervals can be melodic—when notes are played in succession—or harmonic—when notes are played at the same time.

In short, music theory is a powerful tool that can enrich your musical experience. So, whether you are a beginner learning the piano or an experienced musician who wants to deepen music understanding, music theory has a lot to offer you

RCM provides an effective and well-sequenced pathway for developing musical understanding and literacy. Theory studies begin with an introduction to the basic elements of music notation at the elementary level and culminate with structural and harmonic analysis at the advanced levels.

According to Dijak (2021), "Preparatory theory through Level 4 introduces students to the basic elements of music, including notation conventions, melody writing, analysis, and guided listening to selected works from various musical genres and styles."

Levels 5 through 8 build on this foundation, expanding students' knowledge of notation rules, analysis, melody and composition, and music history. This progressive approach ensures that students develop a comprehensive understanding of music theory, preparing them for advanced studies and performance.

Resources for Music Theory

The Royal Conservatory of Music (RCM) offers a range of resources to help students develop their music theory skills, which are crucial for a well-rounded musical education. Here is an overview of the available resources and how they have evolved to better serve students.

The RCM's approach to music theory has transitioned from the earlier Mark Sarnecki's Elementary Music Rudiments book series to the current Celebrate Theory books, which are available from the preparatory level to Level 8. This structured series provides a comprehensive curriculum that aligns with the practical piano exams.

There are no theory exams for Preparatory to Level 4. However, the Celebrate Theory books are designed to build a strong foundation in music theory, ensuring that students develop essential skills early on.

Theory exams become a corequisite for Levels 5 to 8, meaning students must take the corresponding theory exams alongside their piano exams. It is important to keep up with the theory studies for each level to avoid the need to cram all the previous theory content when preparing for Level 5 exams and beyond.

To develop comprehensive reading abilities and musical understanding, the RCM offers the Four-Star Sight Reading and Ear Tests books for levels from Preparatory A to Level 10. These books provide structured exercises that enhance students' sight-reading and ear training skills, which are crucial for practical exams and overall musicianship.

The general rule for sight-reading practice is to use material that is two levels below your current playing level. This approach helps build confidence and proficiency in reading new music quickly and accurately.

Ear Tests help students develop the ability to identify intervals, chords, rhythms, and melodies by ear, which is essential for well-rounded musical development.

The RCM employs an engaging and interactive multimedia learning strategy to prepare students for practical exams. These tools are available online and provide excellent preparation for both sight-reading and ear training. RCM Online Ear Training offers interactive exercises that help students improve their ability to recognize and understand various musical elements by ear. RCM Online Sight Reading provides practice material to enhance students' sight-reading skills, allowing them to approach new pieces with confidence.

In addition to the RCM resources, it is beneficial to start collecting graded material for sight-reading practice. Having a variety of sight-reading books at your disposal can help you build a diverse repertoire and improve your reading skills. The John Kember's Piano Sight-Reading: A Fresh Approach series is specifically designed for sight-reading practice and provides graded material that aligns with your current level. Using such resources can help you develop the habit of regular sight-reading practice, which is crucial for becoming a proficient pianist.

Staying current with music theory and sight-reading is essential for a well-rounded musical education. By utilizing the Celebrate Theory books, Four-Star Sight Reading and Ear Tests books, and interactive online tools provided by the RCM, students can build a solid foundation in music theory and enhance their practical skills. Additionally, incorporating supplementary sight-reading materials into your practice routine will further support your development as a versatile and confident musician.

Unleash the Power of Ear-Training

Ear training is vital in music education and plays a crucial role in the development of the following listening skills:

- **Tone recognition:** It helps musicians identify and differentiate pitches. This is essential for tuning an instrument, singing in tune, and transcribing music.

- **Interval identification:** Intervals are the basis of harmony, and ear training helps musicians recognize these by ear.

- **Rhythmic understanding:** Rhythm is a fundamental component, so understanding and feeling rhythm is basic to keeping time and creating cohesive music.

Also, ear training provides multiple benefits for musicians, such as improved sight-reading, musical memory, and overall musicianship. Let's take a look at each of these terms:

- **Sight-reading:** The ability to read and play music at first sight. This skill helps musicians predict how music will sound based on written notation.

- **Musical memory:** By training the ear to recognize patterns and structures in music, musicians can remember and play pieces of music more accurately. This is especially useful for musicians who play from memory or improvise.

- **Musicianship:** This is the emotional and artistic expression in musical performance. Musicians with a good ear can detect subtleties in music, such as dynamic changes and rhythmic nuances, which they can use to enhance their playing.

A pianist can also improvise through ear training, as it improves understanding of harmony and develops musical intuition. This intuition enables them to make quick and creative decisions, allowing them to predict and respond to changes in the music in real-time.

Ear Training Techniques for RCM Students

Here are some practical tips and resources to improve your ear training:

- Practice regularly: Just like any other skill, ear training improves with regular practice. Try to dedicate a little time each day to ear training exercises.

- Use apps and software: There are many apps and programs that can help you improve your ear training. These can provide you with a wide range of exercises and challenges to keep your practice fresh and interesting; among the most recommended are The Ear Gym and EarMaster.

- Don't just listen to music, but actively listen to it: Try to identify the different elements you hear, such as intervals, scales, chords, and rhythms.

- Try playing or singing the melodies and rhythms you hear: This can help you internalize what you are hearing and improve your ability to recognize these elements in the future.

With patience, practice, and the right resources, you can steadily improve your ear training skills.

Solfeggio Techniques

- First, familiarize yourself with the scale, which is C-D-E-F-G-A-B-C. Each syllable corresponds to a musical note. C is the base note or *key* of the scale.

- Practice the ascending and descending scale, starting by singing the scale ascending— C, D, E, F, G, A, B, C—and then descending—C, B, A, G, F, E, D, C. This will help you become familiar with the sound of each note.

- Use your instrument: Use the piano to play the notes as you sing them. This can help you associate the sound of the note with the corresponding syllable.

- Practice in different keys: Once you feel comfortable singing the scale in one key, try moving to a different key.

- Remember, the goal of solfege is to improve your musical ear and your ability to recognize and reproduce notes. As a recommendation, you can use solfege apps such as Perfect Ear and MyEarTraining.

Ear Training Theory in Action

Music theory and ear training come together when playing the piano; here are real examples:

- Interval recognition: When you play a melody on the piano, you are playing a series of intervals. For example, if you play the C major scale—C, D, E, F, G, A, B, C—you are playing a series of major and minor intervals. With ear training, you can learn to recognize these intervals by their sound, allowing you to play melodies by ear.

- Chord recognition: Chords are a fundamental part of music theory and are used in almost every piece of music. With ear training, you can learn to recognize different types of chords—major, minor, sevenths, etc.—by their sound. This allows you to play chords by ear and also helps you understand the harmonic structure of the pieces you are playing.

- Solfege and sight-reading: Solfege not only helps you improve your musical ear but is also an essential skill for sight-reading. When you see a score, you can use your solfege skills to *hear* the music in your head before you play it. This allows you to play the music more accurately and musically.

- Improvisation and composition: With a good knowledge of music theory and a trained ear, you can begin to improvise and compose your own music. Use your interval and chord recognition skills to create new melodies.

Also, understanding key signatures allows you to quickly identify the key of a piece, which helps you anticipate the notes that are likely to appear. This can make it easier to play and allows you to concentrate on other aspects of playing.

In addition, music theory can influence your phrasing and articulation choices when playing a piece. For example, understanding its harmonic structure can help you decide where to make the pauses—phrasing—and knowing the style and period of it can inform your decisions about how to play the notes—articulation.

So, in this chapter, we have explored the vital importance of music theory and ear training for RCM pianists. These aspects play a crucial role in pianistic development.

The process of refining music literacy is ongoing, and as pianists deepen their understanding, new dimensions open up in their playing. The ability to recognize intervals, chords, and scales aurally not only improves technical accuracy but also enriches artistic expression.

In the next chapter, we will talk about mastering musical skills and explore what the fundamental pillars of music are and their importance in music.

Learning music theory and ear training is an exciting journey. And as we unravel the mysteries of musical language, we discover a deeper appreciation and a more intimate connection to the masterpieces we perform.

Chapter 6

Mastering Musicianship Skills

The music is not in the notes, but in the silence between. –Mozart

In the pursuit of technical perfection, we sometimes forget that music is, first and foremost, a form of emotional expression.

Music has the power to cover a wide range of emotions, from the most exuberant joy to the deepest sadness. It can make us dance with happiness or cry with sorrow. It can comfort us in times of loneliness, and it can intensify our joy in times of celebration.

But how does music manage to convey these emotions? It is not through the notes themselves but through the way they relate to each other. It is the rhythm, melody, harmony, and timbre of the music that speak to us on an emotional level.

Rhythm can make us feel energized or calm. Melody can evoke feelings of nostalgia or anxiety. Harmony can create a sense of tension or tranquility. And timbre, or the color of the music, can give it a unique and distinctive character.

When you play music, try not to focus only on the notes but on the tunes. Feel them. That is the true essence of a musician.

The Pillars of Music

It is important to understand that musicality is not limited to the technical ability to play an instrument. It also includes the ability to understand and communicate the emotion and intention behind the music, which means broadening our understanding of what it means to be musical to include aspects such as creativity and improvisation.

Playing notes correctly is only the starting point in performance. Musicianship also involves expression, which is the ability to transmit feelings and emotions through performance. This can be achieved through dynamics, tempo, and phrasing. In addition, a deeper understanding comes from studying music theory, history, and the cultural context of music. This can enrich performance and allow the musician to connect more meaningfully with the audience.

These concepts support a broader and deeper view of what it means to be a musician, emphasizing the importance of emotional expression, creativity, understanding, and appreciation of music in all its forms.

Among the pillars of music, we can distinguish the most important ones:

Sight-Reading

As mentioned in the previous chapter, it is the ability to read and play music at first sight. This skill helps musicians to predict how the music will sound based on the written notation. Expanding on this concept, we can emphasize that it is the ability to perform an unfamiliar piece of music accurately and fluently from the first time it is seen. It is an essential skill, especially for those playing in orchestras, bands, and chamber ensembles, where they are often expected to play new music with little or no prior rehearsal.

The importance of sight-reading lies in its ability to allow musicians to play unfamiliar pieces with confidence and accuracy. This is especially useful in situations such as auditions, rehearsals, or when presenting a new score. It is also a valuable tool for independent learning and practice.

Here are some practical strategies for improving sight-reading skills:

- **Daily practice:** Just like any other skill, this one improves with regular practice. Try to spend some time each day reading new pieces.

- **Focus on the rhythm first:** Before trying to play all the notes of a piece, try playing just the rhythm. This will help you become familiar with the flow of the music and anticipate rhythm changes.

- **Gradually increase complexity:** Start with simple pieces and gradually increase the difficulty as you become more comfortable. Don't despair if you find a piece particularly challenging; take your time and work on it bit by bit.

- **Analyze the score before playing:** Before you start playing, take a moment to analyze the score. Look for patterns, scales, chords, and key changes; this will give you an idea of what to expect and help you interpret the music more accurately.

- **Practice with a metronome:** A metronome can be a useful tool to keep a steady beat as you practice. Start at a slow tempo and gradually increase the speed as you become more comfortable.

Transposition

Musical transposition consists of "moving a piece of music from one key to another. In other words, it is changing the pitch of the notes of a score without altering its melodic or harmonic structure." By transposing, we maintain a coherent relationship between all the notes, ensuring that the music retains its essence. Note that transposition of one octave is part of theory levels 3–5, and the transposition of any interval within an octave is part of theory level 6.

Benefits of Transposition

- Understanding tonalities: Transposition helps us understand the underlying patterns in tonalities and scales, allowing us to improvise and become more educated musicians. By transposing, we internalize tonal relationships and learn to adapt to different harmonic contexts.

- Facilitates reading: Sometimes, the original key of a piece is outside the range of our instrument. Transposition allows us to bring the music to a level with which we feel comfortable.

- Creates complex arrangements or mashups: If we want to combine our favorite compositions, transposition allows us to adapt them to fit together harmonically. Thus, we can create unique and exciting arrangements.

Transposition can be done in writing by rewriting the score in a new key, applying the necessary accidentals to the notes, or mentally, where experienced musicians can transpose without writing it down. This requires a deep knowledge of tonal relationships. It is a key skill for musicians and practicing it can significantly improve the understanding of harmony and playing in different keys. To master it, it is necessary to study the theory in order to understand tonal relationships and how they apply to transposing, as well as to listen to recordings of transposed pieces to train your ear.

You can perform some specific exercises to help you reach your goal.

Transposing Scales

- Start with diatonic scales in different keys. Play the scale in its original key and then transpose it to other keys. This will help you become familiar with the interval patterns in each scale.

- Practice transposing major scales, minor scales (natural, harmonic, and melodic), and modes (Dorian, Phrygian, Lydian, Mixolydian, and others, which are part of level 8's theory).

Chord Transposition

- Take chord progressions and transpose them to other keys. This will help you understand how chords work in different harmonic contexts.

- Pay attention to chord inversions and how they change when transposing.

- Think of chords in their Roman numeral form before transposing them. This approach provides a clearer understanding of the chord functions and relationships within the progression.

Auditory Skills

Aural skills refer to the ability to perceive, analyze, and understand sound in a musical context. These are very important for musical performance, communication between musicians, and deep appreciation of music.

These skills include:

- **Pitch and intonation:** The ability to recognize and produce accurate notes.
- **Musical dictation:** Translating what is heard into musical notation.
- **Sight-reading:** Performing a score without having previously practiced it.
- **Harmonic analysis:** Identifying chords and progressions.
- **Auditory memory:** Remembering melodies and sound patterns.

Importance of Auditory Skills

- **Sight-reading:** These skills allow you to read and play music without prior preparation. This is essential for studio musicians, orchestras, and choirs.
- **Improvisation:** A good ear helps to improvise melodies and solos with confidence. Listening and responding to harmonic context is key.
- **Understanding harmony:** Auditory skills help us understand how notes interact in chords and progressions.
- **Expressive playing:** A musician with these skills well developed can bring a piece to life with nuance and emotion, distinguishing him or herself from others.

How to Develop Auditory Skills

- **Regular training:** Practice melodic and harmonic dictation exercises.
- **Active listening:** Pay attention to the music you hear. Analyze melodies, rhythms, and harmonies.
- **Sing and play by ear:** Try to reproduce melodies without sheet music.
- **Study music theory:** Understand the relationships between notes and chords.

The RCM program provides learning tools at all levels with over 5,000 exercises and activities in each item to help students develop their auditory recognition, playback, and sight-reading skills for piano. It uses musical examples that allow students to compare their own playing with high-quality professional recordings. It also allows individual progress to be tracked on an ongoing basis.

Performance Techniques

To adequately play the different musical works before them, the performer must be fluent in a series of techniques that allow them to develop their best performance.

Musical interpretation contributes to the understanding and connection with the audience and comprises several points that it is good to break down:

- **The art of musical interpretation:** *Musical interpretation* is "the art of using musical instruments or the voice—the piano, in this case—to generate pleasant and understandable melodies." It is based on knowledge of the musical language, body expression, and the emotion conveyed during performance.

- **The interpreter as a link:** Beyond simply *playing*, the musical interpreter is the link that connects the music with the listeners. The task is to convey it in a way that viewers can grasp it, feel it, and connect with it. Similar to a language translator, the interpreter makes listeners experience the piece in all its senses.

- **Emotional communication:** Interpretation allows emotions to be expressed and communicated. The performer conveys not only the notes but also the message and the story behind the piece. Through proper interpretation, the true meaning of the lyrics, the melody, and the life of the author, are revealed.

Music interpretation is a bridge between the music and the audience, and being a true pianist requires feeling and understanding the music. Therefore, professional training is essential, but also passion and vocation to create an authentic performance.

It is equally important to consider other aspects to have a better performance as a pianist, among them we can mention:

Posture

- Sit upright with your feet flat on the floor.

- Keep your shoulders relaxed and your arms at right angles.

- Avoid neck and back tension.

Relaxation

- Relax your hands and fingers before playing.

- Don't press the keys too hard; allow the muscles to relax between notes.

Articulation

- Touch the keys with precision and clarity.

- Practice legato—connected notes—and staccato—separate notes.

Phrasing

- Express emotions through dynamics and playing.

- Create musical phrases with beginning, development, and ending.

Dynamics

- Vary the intensity of the sound—piano, forte, etc.

- Accentuate important notes to shape the interpretation.

It is also vital to consider some techniques and practical tips for a good presentation:

- **Recognize and accept anxiety:** Anxiety before playing is normal. Accept that it is a natural emotion, and don't judge yourself for feeling it. Remember that even experienced musicians feel nervous before performing.

- **Think like a pro:** Imagine you're on a big stage. Visualize success and satisfaction after playing well. Focus on the music and connecting with your audience instead of worrying about mistakes.

- **Leave the ego behind:** Don't worry about what others think. Play because you love the music and you want to share it. Excessive self-criticism will only increase anxiety.

- **Focus on the task at hand:** Before you play, take a deep breath and concentrate on the present moment. Don't overthink about what could go wrong.

- **Be prepared:** The more confident you feel with the piece, the less anxiety you will have. Rehearse in front of friends or family to get used to playing in front of others.

- **Enjoy the process:** Enjoy every note and every moment on stage. Celebrate your accomplishments, even if they are small.

Now, we can conclude that to play the piano, we must master all the musical skills that make us an integral artist and thus interpret the pieces in a way that transmits to our listeners the true spirit of the compositions. For this, we must have the necessary dedication and not cease in our practices.

And in the search for our identity as musicians, we must have the necessary curiosity to expand our knowledge and, therefore, our horizons.

In the next chapter, we will discuss how to start the path of the RCM method as adults, which is entirely possible and enjoyable. Persevere in the goal of becoming a complete and expressive artist who delights the senses!

Chapter 7

Embarking on the RCM Path as an Adult

It's never too late to be what you might have been. –George Eliot

Meet Robert G., a man who has been passionate about music since he was a kid, especially the piano, but he had never had the opportunity to learn to play it because his studies and work at a very young age had prevented him from doing so. The years passed, but not the desire to create art from that black and white keyboard. Sometimes, his mind used to fly to see himself playing the most beautiful melodies he used to hear. One day, while surfing the internet, he discovered the RCM program. Robert was delighted to see that the RCM offered possibilities for adults.

Intrigued, he decided to enroll in the program. Although he was a bit nervous at first because of his lack of experience, he soon realized he was not alone. There were other adults in the same situation, all eager to learn and grow musically.

The lessons began, and our protagonist immersed himself in the world of the piano. He learned about scales, chords, score reading, and playing techniques. Each week, he practiced diligently, feeling his fingers become more nimble and his musical understanding expand.

The RCM program not only provided him with technical knowledge but also a community of fellow musicians. He joined study groups, attended concerts, and shared his progress with other students. The camaraderie and mutual support motivated him to keep going.

Over time, our pianist managed to play increasingly complex pieces. From classical sonatas to contemporary melodies, his repertoire grew.

One day, in front of an audience of friends and family, he performed a piece he had been practicing for months. The notes flowed with grace and emotion, and at the end, he received a standing ovation. He felt accomplished and grateful for having found the path to his passion belatedly but successfully.

Overcoming Common Concerns

It's important to know that no matter the age, it is never too late to learn to play the piano. However, each stage of adulthood presents unique challenges. Beginners in their '30s, '40s, '50s, and even beyond have been successful in their endeavors. However, it is also true that each adult phase brings its own difficulties.

- **Young adults:** They may struggle to afford lessons—especially if they are newly self-sufficient—and may underestimate the effort and time required in the long run.

- **Middle-aged:** They often struggle to find time in their busy work and family schedules to practice consistently. Sometimes, simply having the energy to practice can seem like a monumental challenge.

- **Seniors:** They may experience concentration problems, interruptions due to health issues, and ingrained habits that make it difficult to acquire good technique.

Despite these obstacles, adult learners also possess personal and situational strengths:

- **Young adults:** They have more time to practice.

- **Middle-aged:** They tend to face fewer financial obstacles and have greater stability.

- **Older students:** They generally do not have family obligations and may have a better understanding of what learning to play a musical instrument really is.

All things being equal, learning to play the piano is no more difficult for adults than it is for children. Most adults can become proficient or even excellent pianists by achieving whatever goals they set for themselves.

Both adults and children have unique advantages in learning to play the piano. Children are a blank canvas, while adults bring self-motivation, self-discipline, and mature cognition.

Juggling Responsibilities

Adult life is often filled with work, family, and personal commitments, making finding time to practice piano tricky. That's why we bring you here some strategies:

- **Shorter, more focused practice sessions:** Instead of long sessions, try practicing for 20–30 minutes a day. Consistency is key.

- **Incorporate practice into your daily routine:** For example, play during your lunch break or before bed.

- **Set realistic goals:** Don't put too much pressure on yourself; progress at your own pace.

Overcome Fear of Failure

It's normal to feel apprehensive, especially if you haven't played the piano in a while. Remember that learning is an ongoing process. Therefore, you must:

- **Maintain a positive mindset:** Focus on the pleasure of learning and growing. Celebrate every small achievement.

- **Learn from success stories:** Listen to inspiring stories of other adults who have thrived in the RCM program. You will see that it is possible.

Relearning

If you have previous piano experience, it's a plus in your favor, and the RCM program can be adapted to your existing knowledge.

- **Identify your strengths and weaknesses:** The program can help you reinforce fundamentals or techniques that may have weakened over time.

- **Placement in the RCM program:** Talk to an instructor to determine the appropriate level based on your previous experience.

Finding the Right Teacher: The Key to Success

Finding a good piano teacher is crucial to learning to play the instrument properly, especially in adulthood, as an experienced piano teacher can help you develop or improve your technical skills, adapt to your level of knowledge to build on your progress, and establish mutually agreed study guidelines.

Clearly, if you study with the RCM method, you must find a certified teacher—an experienced and highly trained professional who will teach you in the right way according to the standards of the program and prepare you for the exams you must take to access higher levels in your learning plan. Through their website, you can immediately have access to a list of them according to your geographic location, as they have more than 30,000 certified teachers throughout North America. You can also ask institutes near your residence or work if there are certified teachers in the RCM method.

You can make a selection based on their experience in teaching adults who have busy lives with work, family, and other obligations. A qualified teacher can adapt lessons to irregular schedules and make the best use of the time available. Teachers should understand your goals and learning style according to your ability and possible limitations. For this reason, sincere and fluid communication between you and the teacher is essential to establish an enriching relationship. You can receive personalized guidance and benefit from their technical teachings, their experience in playing the instrument, and the stories they may have had or have about teaching other adults.

Unlike children, adults see music and the piano from a different perspective. They have established musical tastes and a musical culture of their own that they have cultivated throughout their lives. And beyond the great help and motivation that a teacher can provide, it is not necessary for the teacher to motivate them since they are motivated by their personal desire to learn. That is why it is recommended that they complement their education with online classes or group classes for specific needs; perhaps they have more difficulty learning the theory or have greater difficulties in the technical part or in mastering certain repertoires—with a deeper focus on these aspects, they can master them faster.

Another advantage of being an adult learner is that you can take some control over your piano path. The whole purpose of the book is to give adults information on how the piano journey is structured so they can go into it informed. Children might be fine with just following the instructions of the week, but adults might need to understand the full curriculum to decide if this is something they want to pursue further and to make corrections in their path as needed.

You might not have any real interest in playing classical music. You might hate technical exercises. You might want to do a lot of pieces, or you might want to perfect only a few. You might love or hate theory. If your goal is music production or playing in a band, that is very different from wanting to perform piano concerts. Setting your long-term goals with piano lets you control the direction you are going toward now.

Create a Learning Environment

Set Up Your Space

It is important to set up a space for your study and practice. Dedicate a specific corner in your home for the piano. Even if it's small, having a designated spot will help you focus and create a routine.

- Make sure it is well-lit and ventilated. Natural light is ideal for maintaining concentration.

- Maintain comfort and ergonomics. Use an adjustable stool so you can sit at the right height. Your arms should be parallel to the floor when you play.

- Adopt the correct posture. Sit with your back straight and your feet flat on the floor. This reduces tension and improves comfort.

- Minimize distractions. Turn off electronic devices and avoid distractions such as phones or televisions. Focus on music.

Just because you're not in a formal study environment doesn't mean you shouldn't retain the proper solemnity to carry out your practice, especially if your tutor goes to your house. It is even more important to adapt your environment to provide comfort and a pleasant atmosphere.

Set Realistic Goals and Keep Track of Your Progress

- Establish a regular practice schedule. Consistency is the secret to progress.

- Set clear goals: Define realistic objectives. Some examples might be learning a particular piece, improving a technique, or reaching a certain level.

- Keep a log: Write down your progress. Keeping a practice journal will motivate you and allow you to see your progress over time.

They say that before you learn to run, you have to learn to walk. This phrase extrapolates to any instructional process and should be kept in mind in the process of training to become integral artists.

Join the RCM Community

There are always students who have similar conditions to yours and can bring positive elements to your teaching process. Hence, it is of utmost importance to connect with other students. Look for groups of adult pianists or those who are at a similar level to you. Sharing experiences and advice will inspire you and keep you motivated.

As one of the best study programs nationally and internationally, there is a large number and variety of students who have the same questions or concerns as you. Also, they are willing and eager to communicate and exchange ideas.

You may find some who are a step ahead and can provide you with good advice, or you may find others who have a lower level of knowledge than you, so you may be the one who can support them.

Resources and Strategies for Adult Success

RCM offers a variety of online learning resources for its students of all ages designed to train their skills and knowledge (*Sight Reading*, n.d.). Among the resources, we can find the following:

Elementary Theory Quiz

Students use this quiz to validate their progress on the principles of music theory. A practice quiz is included to demonstrate the types of questions students will experience.

After passing the quiz, students will receive a certificate that is going to be available to download. These are available from preparatory level through level 4.

Online Theory Study Guide and Quizzes

RCM offers interactive practice tests with expertly crafted recommendations that can help students review their understanding and get back on track for success from their homes. These quizzes are available for levels 5–8.

Ear Training and Sight Reading Online

As mentioned previously, these skills are important to train. On its official website, the RCM also offers workshops and summits constantly, as well as concerts of great artists in its facilities throughout the year.

Now, it can be concluded that there is no certain age to learn to play the piano, as long as there is the will to do so and a suitable path is established—any adult who wishes to accomplish this can achieve it.

This is a path traveled in search of a longed-for personal dream, but that is made more bearable and lighter with good company. The RCM method is the ideal way to be the faithful guide on that path until achieving the goals set, thanks to its high quality of teaching through its structured program, its certified teachers, and the wide range of resources it offers.

Part II

Progressing Through the Levels

In this part, we will address two very important chapters, both focused on the progression through the different levels/grades of the Royal Conservatory of Music.

We'll start by briefly explaining the importance of the preparatory stages as well as the piano method levels before moving to the official RCM curriculum.

Expanding in more detail on levels 1–8, we will learn more about the repertoire, ear training, and practice adapted for each RCM level.

Chapter 8

Preparing for the RCM—Piano Method

This chapter equips you with the tools and knowledge necessary to conquer the exciting preparatory stages of the RCM program. We will guide you through piano method levels, establishing a solid foundation in music reading, piano technique, and ear training. Get ready to experience the true joy of playing the piano and confidently approach the advanced levels of the RCM.

Two Popular Piano Methods

Many people assume that a beginner starts at RCM Level/Grade 1, but there is a crucial phase of learning before reaching this milestone. In the Royal Conservatory of Music (RCM) program, this initial phase is comprised of the Preparatory A and Preparatory B levels. Typically, students work through a piano method program before transitioning to the RCM levels.

There are several piano methods available, but the two most commonly used are Alfred's Basic Piano and Faber and Faber's Piano Adventures series. Both methods are highly regarded and come in versions tailored for both adults and children.

Book 1 of both the Adult Piano Adventures and Alfred's Basic Adult Piano Course roughly correspond to Preparatory A in the RCM program. Book 2 for both series is equivalent to Preparatory B. Alfred's also offers a third book in the adult series, which aligns approximately with RCM Level 1.

The Faber and Faber children's series is divided into levels 1A, 1B, 2A, 2B, 3A, 3B, 4, and 5. Alfred's children's series includes levels 1A, 1B, 2A, 2B, 3, 4, and 5.

After completing Books 1 and 2 of the adult piano methods, students have several options: continue with the third book in Alfred's adult series, move to level 3 in Alfred's children's series, transition to level 3A in the Piano Adventures series, or switch to RCM Level 1.

It's important to note that the children's piano method books conclude after level 5, necessitating a switch to the RCM program for continued progression. If you encounter difficulties with RCM Baroque repertoire, as I—Jamie—did, it might be beneficial to continue with the piano method series a bit longer, as they often provide a broader range of material.

Each adult book typically takes six months to a year to complete, so a two-book piano method phase generally lasts between one and two years. In addition to the main series, both Alfred's and Faber and Faber offer supplementary books that can enhance your learning experience. There are also preparatory repertoire books from the RCM, all of which are graded. These supplementary books are excellent for additional practice at your current level and make great sight-reading material as you advance.

During the piano method phase, students typically begin learning scales and technical exercises. Initially, you may not need a dedicated scales book, as the focus will be on pentascales and the major scales of C, G, and F. It is also a good time to start incorporating technical exercises from books such as Burnam's A Dozen A Day, Czerny, or Hanon. These exercises help develop finger strength, independence, and overall technique, laying a solid foundation for future piano studies.

Understanding the importance of the pre-RCM levels and utilizing comprehensive piano method books can significantly enhance a beginner's learning experience. By starting with a structured method, such as Alfred's or Faber and Faber's series, students can build a solid foundation before transitioning to the more advanced RCM levels. Supplementary materials and technical exercises further support this development, ensuring a well-rounded and engaging approach to learning the piano.

When deciding on a piano method for adult learners, both Faber and Faber's Adult Piano Adventures and Alfred's Adult Basic Piano Course offer comprehensive approaches. Each series has its own strengths and can cater to different learning preferences and goals. This section will provide an overview of both methods to help you determine which one might be the best fit for your needs.

Faber and Faber's Adult Piano Adventures series is known for its thorough integration of technique, theory, and repertoire. It provides a well-rounded musical education, making it ideal for students who want a deep understanding of music. The books feature a diverse range of pieces, from classical to contemporary, ensuring that students remain engaged and motivated. The inclusion of familiar songs helps maintain interest. The exercises and pieces are structured to progressively build skills, allowing students to gradually develop their technique and musicality. It is ideal for students who want a comprehensive approach that includes a variety of musical styles and integrates theory and technique with engaging repertoire. It's perfect for those who appreciate a structured progression and multimedia support.

Alfred's Adult Basic Piano Course series is known for its clear, straightforward approach, making it easy for beginners to follow. The explanations are concise and the progression is logical. The course emphasizes practical skills, such as chord playing and sight-reading, which are essential for a wide range of musical styles. The exercises and pieces are carefully graded to ensure that students can progress at a comfortable pace, building confidence as they advance. It is better suited for students who prefer a straightforward, practical approach that emphasizes playing skills and confidence-building. It's ideal for those who want to quickly start playing music and appreciate a clear, easy-to-follow methodology.

Ultimately, the choice between Faber and Faber and Alfred's depends on your personal learning style, goals, and preferences. Both methods provide excellent pathways to developing piano skills, so consider what aspects of learning are most important to you when making your decision.

The Importance of Piano Preparation and Method

Benefits of a Solid Foundation in Music Literacy and Technique

- **Smoother transition:** Having a solid foundation ensures a comfortable and successful transition to official RCM levels. As a result, students who have mastered the basic skills encounter fewer obstacles as they advance in their musical training.

- **Confidence building:** Mastering fundamental skills builds confidence and motivation. As a result, students feel more confident to tackle more complex RCM repertoire.

- **Developing good habits:** From the beginning, both Alfred's and Faber and Faber's piano methods focus on correct posture, hand position, and technique. This helps prevent the formation of bad habits that could hinder future progress.

The Role of the Qualified Piano Teacher

A qualified piano teacher plays a key role in the preparation of pre-RCM students and absolute beginners by providing personalized guidance, correcting technical errors, offering student-specific advice, and primarily motivating a love of music and constant practice.

Core Competencies Prior to RCM

Music Reading

Let's dive into the key skills:

Identification of Notes on the Staff

- **Treble clef and bass clef:** The treble clef is used for the right hand, and the bass clef is used for the left hand. Learn to recognize the notes in both clefs!

- **Lines and spaces:** Each line and space on the staff represents a specific note. For example, in the treble clef, the bottom line is the E note, and the top space is the F note.

Understanding Basic Rhythms

- **Round notes, half notes, and quarter notes:** These rhythmic figures are the basis of all music. Round notes last a full measure, half notes a half measure, and quarter notes one-quarter of a measure.

- **Rests:** In addition to the notes, you must learn the corresponding rests—quarter note rest, eighth note rest, and sixteenth note rest.

Recognition of Single Measures

- **4/4 and 3/4:** The 4/4 time signature is the most common and consists of 4 beats per measure, and 3/4 has 3 beats. Practice feeling the pulse and counting beats while reading sheet music.

To learn to read music, consider sight-reading flashcards. Use flashcards designed specifically for beginners. These feature gradual exercises that will help you recognize notes and rhythms progressively.

Basic Piano Technique

It is important to master the following aspects:

Posture and Hand Position

- **Ergonomics:** Sit upright and relaxed in front of the piano. Keep your shoulders relaxed and your wrists level.
- **Finger curvature:** Fingers should be naturally curved as if you were holding a small ball.

Independence and Coordination of the Fingers

- **Hanon exercises:** Practice scales, arpeggios, and Hanon exercises to strengthen finger independence.
- **Opposing hand:** Work on coordinating the movements of both hands. This is essential for playing more complex pieces.

Remember that skillfully playing the piano is not only a form of artistic expression but also a path to musical health and fluency. Practicing regularly improves memory, concentration, and coordination. However, maintaining proper posture and paying attention to signs of pain to avoid injury is the key to playing fluently while applying the correct technique.

Auditory Training

First, Identify the Simple Intervals

- **Unison and octave:** Unison is the same note, and octave is the same note but in different registers.
- **Differentiate durations:** Listen and differentiate between long and short notes.

Resources for Ear Training   Online Games

Use apps and websites that offer interactive listening exercises. Among some recommended ones are Musictheory.net—a page where you can practice listening intervals; the game consists of listening to different intervals and selecting the correct one—and Session Town—a game more focused on developing a fine-tuned musical ear.

Singing Exercises

Singing simple melodies will help you tune your ear. Here are some recommended exercises that you can implement in your daily practice:

- **Singing intervals:** start with seconds and thirds and then progress to fourths, fifths, and octaves. Also, take a random note on your instrument and sing it, then, from that note, play a major second and sing it along with the instrument.

- **Major scale exercise:** The major scale is an excellent tool for developing the musical ear. You can sing it in different keys and pay close attention to the relationships between the notes and how they sound together.

- **Singing major and minor chords:** Choose simple chords, such as C, G, or F, and pitches. Listen to the quality of the chords and how they relate to the tonic.

These essential skills will prepare you to move forward on your piano journey.

What Is a Piano Method?

A piano method is "a structured program designed to help pianists develop solid musical skills and effectively progress in their piano learning." These methods are especially useful for those with limited or no previous piano experience, as well as those who have been away from the instrument for an extended period of time and need to refresh their basic skills.

Piano Method: A Structured Approach to Learning Piano

A Piano Method program is designed to guide students through a gradual and systematic learning process. Here are some key aspects of the method and how it can benefit developing pianists:

Beginner Starter and Rekindling Skills   This method is ideal for those who are starting from scratch on the piano or for those who need to revive their skills after a period of inactivity. It provides a solid foundation in basic musical concepts, piano technique, and score reading.

Importance of Consistency in Practice   One of the fundamental aspects of successful piano learning is consistency in practice. A Piano Method emphasizes the importance of establishing a regular practice schedule that fits into each student's lifestyle. Regular and consistent practice is key to improving and advancing in piano proficiency.

Setting Realistic Goals   The method encourages students to set realistic and achievable goals for their learning. This includes short-term goals, such as mastering a specific piece or improving a particular technique, as well as long-term goals that encompass progress through the different levels of the method.

Importance of a Good Teacher   As mentioned previously, having a good, qualified teacher is crucial at the preparatory levels of a Piano Method. An experienced teacher can provide expert guidance, correct technical errors, provide constructive feedback, and motivate students to reach their full potential.

Learning Progression Through the Levels

A Piano Method is typically divided into several levels, such as 1A, 1B, 2A, 2B, 3A, and so on. Each level focuses on the progressive development of essential skills, including:

- **Music reading:** Learning to read sheet music effectively, understanding musical notation, and improving the ability to perform new pieces.

- **Basic technique:** Develop a solid technique in hand position, fingering, dynamic control, and musical expression.

- **Ear training:** Improve the ability to listen to and understand music, identify tonal patterns, and develop the musical ear.

Each level of a Piano Method builds on the previous one, providing students with a clear and structured progression in their piano learning.

As you can see, a Piano Method offers a structured and effective approach to learning and improving piano skills. By emphasizing consistency in practice, realistic goal setting, and the guidance of a good teacher, a Piano Method can be a powerful tool for those who wish to master the art of piano.

Conclusion

In this chapter, we have explored the importance of a Piano Method as a fundamental tool for aspiring pianists. We emphasized the need for proper preparation and the building of a solid foundation in basic musical skills and piano techniques.

It is crucial to recognize the positive impact that a well-structured journey through the Royal Conservatory of Music (RCM) levels can have on a pianist's overall success. This gradual, progressive approach ensures a balanced development of technical, interpretive, and aural skills, preparing students to face more complex musical challenges with confidence and skill.

In the next chapter, we will dive into an in-depth, level-by-level discussion of the RCM. We'll explore the specific skills required at each level, the learning objectives, and how pianists can effectively prepare for the RCM certification exams.

Remember that the journey of learning piano is an exciting and rewarding one. Each step along this path brings us closer to realizing our musical potential and the joy of expressing ourselves through this wonderful instrument.

Chapter 9

A Roadmap Through the Levels

I—Adrian—had finally decided to resume my piano learning. When the RCM method was recommended to me, I was intrigued to get information about it in the most complete way possible. However, despite having a well-developed and enjoyable website, I did not find everything I was looking for in one place to start my lessons with a clear vision of the exciting challenge I was facing. So, I had to collect data from various sources and put my puzzle together until I succeeded. Here is the result of all that research so that you, dear reader, can have all the necessary and detailed information about the RCM method for piano and a lot of complementary data and tips.

Below, we will navigate level by level, breaking down each of them. Understanding the structure of the curriculum is important to setting expectations and properly tracking progress.

Level 1

Level 1 of the RCM program marks the beginning of its structured and progressive learning. It focuses on establishing a solid foundation in technique, music reading, and theory, providing the necessary information for continued musical development.

Key Topics

- Development of basic technique: Students will work on developing basic piano techniques, including proper posture, hand position, and independent finger movements.

- Sight-reading skills: Sight-reading music will be introduced, helping students become familiar with sheet music and improve their ability to perform new pieces accurately.

- Music theory: Basic concepts of music theory will be addressed, such as note reading, rhythm, and some intervals, laying the foundation for a deeper understanding of music and its structure.

Repertoire

The repertoire in level 1 encompasses a variety of pieces carefully selected to develop technical and musical skills. Some examples of composers and styles that students can expect include:

Musical Style: Baroque–Classical

- **Composer:** Georg Philipp Telemann.
- **Work:** "Fantasia in G Minor, TWV 33:17"—with repetition.
- **Source:** You can find this music in the "12 Little Fantasies."
- **Characteristics and purpose:** This Baroque piece is not very complicated and is ideal to begin to familiarize yourself with a more independent left hand on the piano.

Musical Style: Romantic–20th Century

- **Composer:** Dmitri Kabalevsky.
- **Work:** "Waltz, op. 39 no. 13."
- **Source:** You can find this music in the "24 Pieces for Children."
- **Characteristics and purpose**: This beautiful minor key waltz features a steady rhythm of thirds in the left hand and a soaring, expressive right hand. It is a great introduction to the world of waltzes.

Musical Style: Modern

- **Composer:** Marta Mier.
- **Play:** "Sneaky Business."
- **Source:** You can find this music in the book *Jazz, Rags and Blues, Book 1.*
- **Characteristics and purpose**: Martha Mier's music is enjoyable and generally gets even the most demanding students to practice her compositions. "Sneaky Business" can be an excellent introduction to walking bass lines—it's a very *cool* sound for this level!

Musical style: Inventions

- **Composer:** Galán, Pierre.
- **Play:** "Una pequeña canción entre amigos."
- **Source:** Imitations and inventions.
- **Features and purposes:** This piece is a good starting point for inventions. Inventions are the ultimate study of hand independence, and there is a simple back-and-forth quality to this piece. Try to achieve uninterrupted phrasing as it changes from hand to hand.

It is crucial to select a repertoire that appeals to the student's interest and is in line with the teacher's recommendations. Variety in repertoire helps to develop technical and expressive skills from the beginning.

Technical Studies

The focus in level 1 technical studies is on the development of solid, basic techniques. This includes working on proper playing posture, hand position to facilitate fluid movements, finger independence for accurate playing, and practice of basic scales and arpeggios. Examples of technical studies include 2-octave major scales and arpeggios in C, F, and G major.

Theory and Auditory Training

At this level, fundamental music theory concepts are introduced, such as basic note reading, understanding of rhythm, and recognition of simple intervals. Basic aural skills such as identification of aural intervals and differentiation of rhythmic patterns also begin to develop.

Musical Dexterity

Level 1 also focuses on musical dexterity, addressing aspects such as clear articulation of notes and the development of basic musical phrasing to express emotions and nuances in interpretation.

Weekly Sample Practice Schedule

Main Objectives

- to establish a solid foundation in basic piano technique

- to become familiar with music reading and basic theory concepts

- to develop basic musical dexterity and initial listening skills

Time Distribution:

Repertoire and Works

- Basic repertory—elementary level music: 60 minutes.

- Pieces from the "Celebration Series, Piano Repertoire" and selections from "Piano Adventures."

- Sight reading exercises: 20 minutes.

- You can use "Four-Star Sight Reading and Ear Tests" to improve your music reading.

Technical Studies

- 2-octave major scales in C, F, and G major: 20 minutes

- basic arpeggios in C, F, and G major: 10 minutes

Theory and Auditory Training

- basic note and rhythm reading: 15 minutes

- identification of simple auditory intervals: 10 minutes

Musical dexterity

- proper posture and hand position: 10 minutes

- articulation and basic phrasing: 10 minutes

Breaks and Review

- short breaks between sessions: 10 minutes

- review and consolidation of what has been learned: 15 minutes

Total Practice Time: 3 Hours Per Week

It is important to dedicate time to repertoire as well as technical studies and music theory for a balanced development in RCM level 1. The additional resources mentioned below can be of great help in strengthening musical skills in a comprehensive manner.

Additional Resources

- "Celebration Series, Piano Repertoire" by RCM.

- "Four-Star Sight Reading and Ear Tests" by RCM.

- "Piano Adventures" by Nancy and Randall Faber.

- "Music for Little Mozarts" by Christine H. Barden, et al.

Level 2

Level 2 of the RCM program is a progression from the previous level, where students consolidate and expand their technical, theoretical, and expressive skills. This level prepares students to explore more diverse and challenging repertoire while strengthening their musical understanding and creativity.

Key Topics

- Development of basic technique: Continued work on posture, hand position, finger independence, and fluency in scales and arpeggios.

- Sight-reading skills: Progress is made in music reading with more complex scores and varied rhythms.

- Music theory: Introduces more advanced concepts of theory, including basic musical forms and harmonic structures.

Repertoire

Musical Style: Baroque–Classical

- **Composer:** Beethoven, Ludwig van.

- **Work:** "Ecossaise in G major, WoO 23."

- **Source:** imslp.org, Dances for Piano and the *RCM 2 Repertoire Book*.

- **Characteristics and purpose**: Similar to Mozart's K2 in that there are appoggiaturas that create a fun syncopation. This one is more challenging and faster. It is also good practice with the broken I and V7 chords.

Musical Style: Romantic–20th Century

- **Composer:** Grechaninov, Alexandr T.

- **Work:** "Farewell, op. 98 no. 4."

- **Source:** *Children's Album, op. 98—sheet music plus*; imslp.org

- **Characteristics and purpose**: This piece has a good amount of left-hand movement, and you will get some practice with the dotted crotchet and 2 bar slurs to practice expressive phrasing.

Musical Style: Modern

- **Composer:** Norton, Christopher.

- **Play:** "Tango Toronto."

- **Source:** *Christopher Norton Connections 2—score more.*

- **Features and purpose**: If you are interested in Tango, this is a fun challenge. It is an excellent introduction to this spicy style.

Musical Style: Inventions

- **Composer:** Richert, Teresa.

- **Play:** "Brave Cat."

- **Source:** *RCM 2 Repertory Book.*

Features and purposes: This piece is a good starting point for inventions. Inventions are the ultimate study of hand independence, and there is a simple back-and-forth quality to this piece. Try achieving uninterrupted phrasing as it changes from hand to hand.

Technical Studies

Similar to level 1, the technical focus is on consolidating proper posture, efficient hand position, and independent finger movements. Major and minor scales, arpeggios, and specific technical patterns are practiced to strengthen technique and fluency at the keyboard.

Theory and Auditory Training

Students explore more advanced music theory concepts, such as complex note reading, varied rhythms, extended intervals, and understanding of basic musical forms. In addition, emphasis is placed on ear training to improve auditory recognition skills and musical comprehension.

Musical Dexterity

Musical skills are continually developed, focusing on expressiveness, proper dynamics, clear articulation, and musical phrasing to convey emotion and nuance in interpretation.

Weekly Sample Practice Schedule

Main Objectives

- Expand technical, theoretical, and expressive skills.

- Explore a wider and more diverse repertoire.

- Continue to develop musical proficiency and advanced listening skills.

Time Distribution:

Repertoire and Works

- Works by Turk, Haydn, Beethoven, and Mozart: 60 minutes. Include sonatinas, minuets, burlesques, bourrées, écossaises, and gavottes, among others.

- Sight reading exercises: 20 minutes. Use "Four-Star Sight Reading and Ear Tests" to improve music reading.

Technical Studies

- advanced major and minor scales: 20 minutes. In keys such as D, B flat, A minor, E minor, etc.

- advanced arpeggios: 10 minutes. Including seventh arpeggios

Theory and Auditory Training

- advanced note reading and rhythm: 15 minutes

- advanced interval recognition: 10 minutes

Musical Dexterity

- posture and hand position refinement: 10 minutes

- musical expression and advanced dynamics: 10 minutes

Breaks and Review

- short breaks between sessions: 10 minutes

- review and consolidation of what has been learned: 15 minutes

Total Practice Time: 3 Hours Per Week

As you can see, this schedule focuses on expanding the skills acquired in level 1 and prepares you to tackle a more diverse and challenging repertoire. It is crucial to dedicate time to repertoire and technical studies, music theory, and musicianship for a balanced development in RCM level 2.

Additional Resources

- "Celebration Series, Piano Repertoire Level 2" from the RCM.

- RCM's "Four-Star Sight Reading and Ear Tests Level 2."

- RCM's "Technical Requirements for Piano Level 2."

- "Alfred's Basic Piano Library Level 2" by Willard A. Palmer, Morton Manus, and Amanda Vick Lethco.

Level 3

The third level of the RCM program represents a significant advancement in students' pianistic ability. By moving into more complex and extended sonatinas, students reach a crucial developmental point in their musical journey. This level serves as a bridge to higher levels, where the material, although more challenging, becomes less intimidating due to the solid foundation established in previous levels.

Key Topics

- Development of skills in Baroque and classical dances: Students delve into the interpretation and performance of Baroque and classical dances, exploring styles such as minuets, gavottes, and sarabandas.

- Understanding the structure of sonatinas: The structure and form of sonatinas are introduced, allowing students to approach longer and more complex works.

- Exploration of sonata and composite form: We begin to explore the structure and characteristics of sonata form, as well as composite composition.

- Development of advanced scale, arpeggio, and chord techniques: Students advance in the mastery of scales and arpeggios in major and minor keys, and dominant seventh chords are introduced.

- Introduction to complex rhythms and dynamics in terraces: Advanced rhythms such as 6/8, 12/8, 7/8, and 5/4 are covered, along with dynamics in terraces for a more expressive interpretation.

- Expansion of knowledge of intervals, interval inversions, and cadences: Students deepen their understanding of intervals and cadences, as well as interval inversions.

- Introduction to music writing and understanding key composers: Basic music writing is introduced, and key composers such as Bach, Clementi, Handel, Schumann, Bartok, and Grechaninov are explored.

Repertoire

Musical Style: Baroque

- **Composer:** Purcell, Enrique.

- **Work:** "Hornpipe in B flat major, Z 685."

- **Source:** Essential Keyboard Repertoire 4 (sheetmusicplus).

- **Characteristics and purpose:** It is important to learn to disconnect beats 2 and 3 to really generate the joyful feeling of this dance—hornpipe. Practice the right hand just to get a real feel for this and study the bagpipe while you do it.

Musical Style: Classical

- **Composer:** Clementi, Muzio.

- **Work:** "Sonatina in C major, op. 36 no. 1"—any movement.

- **Source:** Six progressive sonatinas for strong piano, op.36 (sheet music plus), RCM Repertoire level 3.

Characteristics and Purpose The first movement of this sonatina is on the list of essential exercises for every pianist. If you are tackling your first sonatina, it is crucial that you master the fundamental concepts of sonata form, which include exposition, development, and recapitulation. Sonatinas, while challenging, offer an excellent opportunity to work on technical exercises such as scales, broken chords, and others.

In contrast, the second movement is simpler and slower. Here, the challenge is to keep the left-hand chord patterns smooth, allowing the right hand to soar fluidly. Finally, the third movement features interesting passages, such as sixteenth notes, rhythms, and driving sequences, as well as slurs, dynamic changes, and scale passages. This movement is an opportunity to explore expressiveness and variety in musical interpretation.

Musical style: Romantic–20th Century

- **Composer:** Tchaikovsky, Piotr Il'yich.
- **Work:** "Morning Prayer, op. 39 no. 1."
- **Source:** Albúm para los jóvenes, op.39 (scores plus), Repertorio RCM level 3.

Characteristics and purpose: Liturgical chorales are difficult to play on the piano. You must move smoothly from chord to chord while all the notes of your chords sound simultaneously. You must also emphasize the melody of the top—soprano—note, which is no small feat in 4-part writing.

Musical Style: Modern

- **Composer:** Norton, Christopher.
- **Work:** "White sand."
- **Source:** Christopher Norton's Connections for Piano 3 (score plus).
- **Characteristics and purpose:** The delicious tropical flavor of calypso in this composition is highly appealing, but the rhythm poses a considerable challenge. At times, the left hand and right hand perform very different actions: This becomes an excellent exercise in exploring syncopation and hand independence.

Musical Style: Studies

- **Composer:** Donkin, Christina.
- **Work:** "Witches and Wizards."
- **Source:** Legends and Traditions (scores plus), RCM Studies Level 3.

Characteristics and purpose: This composition is exciting when played in a 6/8 time signature, and its character is intensely stormy. Memorizing this piece can be done quickly if you can identify the patterns; use your knowledge of chords to do this. In addition, the piece is divided into two distinct sections.

Technical Studies

Technical studies at this level focus on the continued development of scales and arpeggios in major and minor keys, the incorporation of dominant seventh chords, and the practice of complex rhythms such as 6/8, 12/8, 7/8, and 5/4. Specific exercises include scales in Bb,

A, Eb, and minor keys such as Bm, Dm, Gm, and Cm, along with arpeggios of dominant seventh chords.

Theory and Auditory Training

At this level, the understanding of major, minor, augmented, and diminished intervals, as well as interval inversions and cadences is deepened. Music writing concepts such as SATB, cadences, and basic question-and-answer composition are addressed, along with a greater emphasis on ear training to recognize and reproduce complex melodies and rhythms.

Musical Dexterity

Students will work on terraced dynamics for more expressive interpretation, Alberti bass, and transposition of melodies to develop accompaniment skills and understanding of musical structures. Letter writing within musical notation will also be initiated as part of understanding musical context and expression.

Weekly Sample Practice Schedule

Main Objectives

- Improve the interpretation of sonatinas and works by key composers.
- Master advanced technical studies and complex rhythms.
- Deepen in music theory and ear training.
- Develop musical composition and writing skills.

Time Distribution: Repertoire and Works

- sonatinas (2): 50 minutes
- works by key composers: 30 minutes
- style pieces: 20 minutes

Technical Studies

- advanced scales and arpeggios in major and minor keys: 30 minutes
- dominant seventh chords and complex rhythms (6/8, 12/8, etc.): 20 minutes

Theory and Auditory Training

- intervals, cadences, and musical writing: 20 minutes
- ear training exercises for complex rhythms and melodies: 15 minutes

Musical Dexterity

- terrace dynamics and transposition of melodies: 15 minutes

- letter composition within the musical notation: 10 minutes

Breaks and Review

- breaks between practice sessions: 10 minutes

- review and consolidation of what has been learned: 15 minutes

Total Practice Time: 3 Hours Per Week

It is important to maintain a balance between technical practice, repertoire performance, theoretical development, and musical creativity, for comprehensive progress in RCM Level 3.

Additional Resources

- Works by Mozart, Beethoven, and other composers in sonata form

- *Piano Études Level 3 Book, 2015 Edition*

- *Royal Conservatory Celebration Series*, from the RCM

Level 4

Level 4 of the RCM program marks a significant stage in the musical development of piano students. It focuses on progression into a more complex repertoire and sophisticated rhythms, especially within the context of the Romantic and Modern repertoire. Students are faced with more advanced technical and theoretical challenges, preparing them to face works of greater musical and expressive depth.

Key Topics

- Development of advanced skills in Baroque and classical dance: Students will work on the interpretation and musical expression of Baroque and classical works with a focus on articulation, phrasing, and dynamics.

- In-depth understanding of the structure of sonatinas and sonata forms: The formal structure of sonatinas and sonata forms is explored in detail, including exposition, development, recapitulation, and coda.

- Exploration of major and minor keys, as well as dominant seventh chords: Students expand their understanding of keys and chords, including the role of dominant seventh chords in harmonic progressions and cadences.

- Mastery of complex rhythms and beat groupings: Advanced rhythms and beat groupings are worked on to improve rhythmic precision and fluency in interpretation.

- Development of the Alberti bass technique and terraced dynamics: Focuses on the Alberti bass technique to create complex piano textures and practice terraced dynamics to achieve an expressive and controlled interpretation.

Repertoire

Musical Style: Baroque

- **Composer:** Bach, Carl Philipp Emanuel.

- **Work:** "March in D major, BWV Anh. 122".

- **Source:** Notebook for Anna Magdalena Bach, imslp.org, RCM Repertoire Level 4.

- **Characteristics and purpose:** In relation to marching, what are the key aspects? Mainly, it is essential to master a solid quarter-note rhythm. Unlike conventional marches, here we find a small syncopation. This challenge involves complex manual independence, which makes it an excellent exercise to practice with the hands separately.

Musical Style: Classical

- **Composer:** Clementi, Muzio.

- **Work:** "Sonatina in G major, op. 36 no. 3 third movement."

- **Source:** Six progressive sonatinas for strong piano, op. 36 (sheet music plus), imslp.org, RCM Repertoire Level 4.

- **Characteristics and purpose:** The second movement of the piece is beautiful and slow, with a steady dotted melody. At one point, the right and left hands exchange roles, and the right hand becomes the accompaniment. The third movement is fast and full of contrasts. Scales move in both directions, and zigzag patterns are presented, among other elements. The real challenge lies in keeping the left hand quiet while the right-hand melody plays expressive phrases over the top. One suggestion for practicing this setup is to play the melody with blocked chords.

Musical style: Romantic–20th Century

- **Composer:** Schumann, Robert.

- **Work:** "The Wild Rider, op. 68 no. 8."

- **Source:** *Album for Young People*, op. 68, imslp.org.

- **Characteristics and purpose:** This composition is highly vigorous and, in addition, enjoys great popularity within Schumann's *Album for Young People*. It is presented as an excellent exercise for practicing chord progressions, including the i-iv-V and IV chords. In addition, the left hand requires special attention to the melodic aspect, and the piece has many chords.

This is an excellent example of blues for those who don't know the genre well: Its rhythm is slow and steady and creates an impressive mood. The rhythm oscillates in a simple way. Some chords played with the left hand can be challenging, but this piece serves as a wonderful introduction to the blues.

Musical Style: Studies

- **Composer:** Czerny, Carl.
- **Work:** "Étude in E major, op. 139 no. 66."
- **Source:** 100 progressive exercises, op. 139, imslp.org, RCM Studies Level 4.
- **Characteristics and purpose:** This sophisticated, moderately paced piece focuses on an Alberti bass pattern played with the left hand. It offers ample opportunities for expression, and it is valuable to explore the chords employed in it.

Technical Studies

- The learning of major and minor keys is deepened, including arpeggios with separated hands to improve the coordination and independence of the fingers.
- The understanding of the seventh dominant chords and their application in harmonic progressions are initiated.

Theory and Auditory Training

- Minor, augmented, and diminished intervals are explored in detail, as well as interval inversions and their relationship to 4-note chords.
- Work is done on aural identification and understanding of more complex harmonic structures.

Musical Dexterity   It focuses on the refinement of musical interpretation, including terraced dynamics and Alberti bass technique, to achieve an expressive and nuanced performance.

Weekly Sample Practice Schedule
Main Objectives

- technical and expressive mastery in sonatinas and romantic–modern repertoire
- deepening the understanding of sonata structures and advanced musical forms
- development of aural and theoretical skills to approach complex repertoire

Time Distribution:

Repertoire and Works

- Advanced repertoire—sonatinas, romantic/modern works: 60 minutes. Include pieces by Clementi, Schumann, Czerny, and others, that present technical and expressive challenges.
- Sight reading exercises: 20 minutes.

Technical Studies

- advanced scales and arpeggios in all major and minor keys: 30 minutes

- specific studies to address technical difficulties in the selected works: 30 minutes

Theory and Auditory Training

- theoretical analysis of the selected works: 15 minutes

- advanced auditory training—identification of chords and complex harmonic structures: 15 minutes

Musical Dexterity

- Detailed musical performance of the selected works: 30 minutes.

- Focus on dynamics, articulation, and expression to achieve a nuanced and emotional performance.

Breaks and Review

- short breaks between sessions: 10 minutes

- review and consolidation of what has been learned: 20 minutes

Total Practice Time: 3 Hours Per Week

It is essential to devote significant time to advanced repertoire, specific technical studies, and theoretical analysis in order to comprehensively address the musical demands of this level. Regular breaks and reviews are essential to maintain freshness and progress in musical practice.

Additional Resources

- Clementi Sonatinas

- Anna Magdalena Bach's notebook

- Collections of Schumann, Bartok, and Grechaninov

- Recommendation to listen to sonatas by Mozart and Beethoven to understand sonata form in context

Level 5

At RCM level 5, students advance significantly in their piano development, facing more challenging repertoire, advanced technical studies, and a greater depth in music theory. This level represents a crucial point on the road to piano mastery.

Key Topics

- Advanced technique development: Emphasis is placed on the importance of an ergonomic and relaxed posture when playing the piano, mastery of fingering, including the proper use of the fingers to achieve precise and effortless technical execution, especially in fast and complex passages, and finally, time is dedicated to exploring and perfecting musical dynamics, including volume gradation and expressiveness in interpretation to communicate emotions and musical nuances effectively.

- Sight-reading skills: Students will practice interpreting scores that involve advanced musical elements, such as rapid tempo changes, key changes, and complex textures, thus improving their ability to approach challenging repertoire with accuracy and fluency. Students will work on increasing the speed of score reading and developing the ability to recognize and process musical information more quickly and efficiently. Finally, they will practice the instant identification of melodic, harmonic, and rhythmic patterns in the scores, which facilitates the fluid interpretation and anticipation of the music.

- In-depth study of music theory: A detailed analysis of complex harmonic structures, such as extended chord progressions, remote modulations, and chromaticism techniques, will be carried out, thus developing a deep understanding of harmony in music. Musical forms such as rondos and variations will be studied, analyzing their structure and specific characteristics, which broadens the student's knowledge of the organization and development of music at a macro-structural level.

Repertoire

Musical Style: Baroque

- **Composer:** Bach, Johaan Sebastian.

- **Work:** "Little Prelude in C major, BWV 939."

- **Source:** Little Preludes, imslp.org.

- **Characteristics and purpose:** This piece is an introduction to Bach's Little Preludes and is an important and serious step on the road to learning the Baroque. The left hand's initial octave in C serves as a pedal point and has a majestic organ-like quality.

Musical style: Classical

- **Composer:** Mozart, Wolfgang Amadeus.

- **Work:** "Minuet and Trio, Viennese Sonatina no. 1."

- **Source:** Viennese Sonatinas, imslp.org.

- **Characteristics and purpose:** This composition begins simply enough, but the B section is challenging: It features ascending thirds in both hands, some ascending sixths, and numerous leaps. It serves as an excellent introduction to more challenging classical music, such as more complex sonatinas or simpler sonatas.

Musical style: Romantic–20th Century

- **Composer:** Greig, Edvard.

- **Work:** "Waltz, op. 12 no. 2."

- **Source:** Lyrical pieces, imslp.org.

- **Characteristics and purpose:** This is one of the most accessible lyrical compositions to try. The waltz pattern played with the left hand requires considerable stretching, and it takes some time to become familiar with the main melodic figure; it is quite atypical. Don't be intimidated by the length of this piece: it's quite repetitive.

Musical Style: Modern

- **Composer:** Gillock, William L.

- **Work:** "Nightfall in New Orleans."

- **Source:** New Orleans Jazz Styles.

- **Characteristics and purpose:** This piece starts slow and has an improvisational and wandering character. It contains some rich and appealing jazz chords to experiment with. Subsequently, an infectious rhythm is introduced accented with intermittent chords, before returning to our slower section, now with more depth and some additional octaves.

Musical Style: Studies

- **Composer:** Burgmüller, Johann Friedrich.

- **Work:** "Dulce dolor, op. 100 no. sixteen."

- **Source:** Vingt-cinq études faciles et progressives, op. 100, imslp.org, RCM Studies Level 5.

- **Features and purpose:** If you are focusing your efforts on improving your hand balance, this étude is ideal for you. It features a prominent melody, while the accompaniment remains on a secondary level. The étude employs a fragmented chord accompaniment to convey a sense of sadness, complemented by a descending melody.

Technical Studies

Technical studies in level 5 focus on perfecting advanced techniques, including scales in less common keys and extended chord arpeggios. Specific exercises are worked on to improve coordination, speed, and agility at the keyboard.

Theory and Auditory Training

Music theory is explored in depth with detailed score analysis and advanced theoretical concepts. Ear training focuses on identifying complex intervals, recognizing modulations, and understanding sophisticated harmonic structures.

Musical Dexterity

Level 5 seeks to perfect musical dexterity through impeccable technical execution, expressive interpretation, and total control over dynamics and phrasing. It works on emotional expressiveness and connection with the music.

Weekly Sample Practice Schedule

Main Objectives

- improvement of advanced technique and musical expressiveness

- improved sight-reading of complex scores

- deepening in the analysis and understanding of advanced music theory

Time Distribution:

Repertoire and Works

- Advanced repertoire—intermediate-advanced music: 60 minutes.

- Sight-reading exercises: 20 minutes. The interpretation of complex scores is recommended to improve accuracy and fluency in music reading.

Technical Studies

- Advanced scales and arpeggios: 30 minutes. Includes scales in less common keys and extended chord arpeggios.

- Dynamics and musical expression: 20 minutes. Work on dynamics and expressiveness for a more emotional and expressive musical interpretation.

Theory and Auditory Training

- Advanced harmonic analysis: 15 minutes. It is recommended to study complex harmonic structures and modulations.

- Recognition of musical patterns: 15 minutes. A focus on the instant identification of melodic and rhythmic patterns in sheet music is recommended.

Musical Dexterity

- Advanced posture and fingering: 15 minutes. Although at a more advanced level, it is recommended to practice posture refinement, hand position, and fingering control.

- Expression and dynamics: 15 minutes. Work on dynamics and musical expression to communicate emotions in performance.

Breaks and Review:

- short breaks between sessions: 10 minutes

- review and consolidation of what has been learned: 15 minutes

Total Practice Time: 3 Hours Per Week

This schedule focuses on honing advanced technical skills, music reading of complex works, and a thorough understanding of music theory. It is important to dedicate time to both challenging repertoire and technical studies and theory for comprehensive development at RCM level 5.

Additional Resources

- *The Art of Piano Playing* by Heinrich Neuhaus

- *Piano Technique* by Walter Gieseking

- *Fundamentals of Piano Practice* by Chuan C. Chang

- sonatas and advanced works by composers such as Beethoven, Brahms, Rachmaninoff, and Liszt

- *Tonal Harmony* by Stefan Kostka and Dorothy Payne

Level 6

RCM level 6 is a crucial milestone on the path of pianistic development, marked by the consolidation of advanced technical and theoretical skills. Students explore a diverse and complex repertoire, allowing them to deepen their musical understanding and artistic expressiveness.

Key Issues

- Advanced technical development: The focus will be on perfecting posture, finger independence, and the precise execution of scales, arpeggios, and chords in more complex keys.

- Music reading skills and advanced theory: Students advance in the interpretation of complex scores and deepen theoretical concepts such as modes, advanced chords, and compositional techniques.

- Exploration of a diversified and complex repertoire: We will work on works by renowned composers, addressing Baroque dance suites, classical forms, and virtuosic works of different styles and periods.

Repertoire

Musical style: Baroque

- **Composer:** Bach, Johaan Sebastian.
- **Work:** "Little Prelude in E minor, BWV 941."
- **Source:** Little Preludes.imslp.org. RCM Repertoire Level 6.
- **Characteristic and purpose:** This little prelude is quite complex. Two main elements occur in it: a repeating arpeggiated figure and suspensions–resolutions that are repeated in the upper voices. The suspensions are a melodic technique that deserves to be studied due to its great expressiveness. In addition, this composition presents a piquancy at the conclusion.

Musical Style: Classical

- **Composer:** Clementi, Muzio
- **Work:** "Any movement, sonatina in F major, op. 36 no. 4."
- **Source:** Six progressive sonatinas for strong piano, op. 36, imslp.org.
- **Features and purpose:** The entire sonatina consists of three movements and lasts approximately eight minutes. As with all of Clementi's sonatinas, you will find numerous playful and fun figures, fast notes, vibrant octaves, etc. Classical compositions are often among the most challenging at any grade/level.

Musical style: Romantic–20th Century

- **Composer:** Greig, Edvard.
- **Work:** "Arieta, op. 12 no. 1."
- **Source:** Piezas líricas, imslp.org
- **Features and purpose:** It is an excellent study on multi-voice playing, in which each hand plays one or two voices at a time.

Musical Style: Modern

- **Composer:** Gillock, William L.
- **Play:** *Winter Scene.*
- **Source:** Lyrical preludes in romantic style.

- **Characteristics and purpose:** This triple-meter musical work alternates the melody between the hands and has a mysterious charm that is very appealing. Throughout the piece, truly fascinating chord choices are presented.

Musical Style: Studies

- **Composer:** Czerny, Carl.

- **Work:** "Étude in A flat major, op. 139 no. 51."

- **Source:** 100 progressive exercises, op. 139, imslp.org, sixth-level RCM studies.

- **Characteristics and purpose:** Like many of the compositions I suggest to my students in this level, this étude focuses on the balance between the hands: a lyrical melody in the right hand that overlays the left-hand accompaniment. There is a pedal for the left-hand finger and some ornaments and turns for the right hand.

Technical Studies

Technical studies focus on technical refinement through exercises that strengthen advanced posture, finger independence, and the fluid execution of scales, arpeggios, and chords in various keys and keyboard positions.

Theory and Auditory Training

Music theory is deepened with the introduction of advanced concepts such as modes, extended chords, and compositional techniques. Ear training focuses on recognizing complex chords, transposition, and advanced score reading.

Musical Dexterity

Level 6 prioritizes artistic refinement, including emotional expression through advanced phrasing, expressive articulation, and mature interpretation of selected works.

Weekly Sample Practice Schedule

Main Objectives

- Consolidate advanced technical skills.

- Deepen in musical interpretation and artistic expressiveness.

- Develop a deep understanding of advanced music theory.

Time Distribution:

Repertoire and Works

- Diversified and complex repertoire: 60 minutes daily. Includes works by composers such as Gillock, Clementi, or Edvard.

- Advanced sight-reading exercises: 20 minutes daily. Interpretation of complex scores with increased accuracy and fluency is recommended.

Technical Studies Advanced technical refinement: 30 minutes daily. Exercises can be performed to perfect posture, finger independence, scales, and arpeggios in complex keys.

Theory and Auditory Training

- In-depth study of advanced music theory: 20 minutes daily. This includes analysis of advanced harmonic structures, modulations, and complex musical forms.

- Advanced ear training: 20 minutes daily. This includes complex chord recognition, transposition, and advanced score reading.

Musical dexterity Advanced musical expression and phrasing: 30 minutes daily. A focus on mature and emotional interpretation of selected works is recommended.

Breaks and Review

- short breaks between sessions: 10 minutes

- review and consolidation of what has been learned: 15 minutes per day

Total Practice Time: 3 Hours Per Week

It is important to maintain a balance between technical practice, expressive interpretation, and theoretical study for an integral development as a level 6 RCM pianist.

Additional Resources

- *Harmony and Voice Leading* by Edward Aldwell and Carl Schachter.

- *The Study of Orchestration* by Samuel Adler.

- *Advanced Piano Technique* by Alan Fraser.

- *The Art of Piano Performance* by Heinrich Neuhaus.

- *Piano Technique* by Walter Gieseking and Karl Leimer.

Level 7

Level 7 of the RCM Program marks a crucial point in the student's pianistic evolution, moving into early advanced repertoire and focusing on mastery of hand independence and interpretive subtlety.

Key Topics

- Development of hand independence: Intensive work on coordination and independent control of both hands for more complex and expressive performances.

- In-depth study of Bach's Two-Part Inventions and Beethoven's Bagatelles: Detailed analysis and practice of works that demand technical precision and deep musical understanding.

- Study of 12 Bar Blues and classical symphonies: Exploration of diverse styles to broaden the interpretative palette and understanding of complex musical structures.

Repertoire

Musical Style: Baroque

- **Composer:** Händel, George Friedrich.

- **Work:** "4th movement: Aria, Suite No. 8 in G major, HWV 441."

- **Source:** Piano Suites 1733, imslp.org.

- **Characteristics and purpose:** Normally, arias are singable melodies, but this one is exceptionally ornate and unusual. The right hand carries the heaviest workload, while the left hand focuses primarily on individual notes that must be played independently. It is important to pay attention to cadences and make a slight crescendo as you progress through the piece.

Musical Style: Classical

- **Composer:** Beethoven, Ludwig van.

- **Work:** "Fur Elise, WoO 59."

- **Source:** Beethoven's Piano Pieces, imslp.org, RCM Repertoire Level 7.

- **Characteristics and purpose:** This is one of the most recognized piano compositions in history. The opening section—the most popular—is fairly straightforward; it is the second and third parts that present the most challenges. This bagatelle offers great diversity and is a delight to learn.

Musical Style: Romantic–20th Century

- **Composer:** Kabalevsky, Dmitri.

- **Work:** "Rondo-March, op. 60 no. 1."

- **Source:** Four Rondos, op. 60.

- **Characteristics and purpose:** The four Rondo-type compositions in this collection correspond to a seventh-level level and are worthy of investigation. These works can be used for the study of the Rondo structure. You may find these pieces intimidating until you identify the musical phrase. As with any march, it is essential to maintain a solid rhythmic pulse.

Musical Style: Modern

- **Composer:** Bonsor, Brian.
- **Play:** *Feeling good.*
- **Source:** Jazz Piano 2.
- **Characteristics and purpose:** It is important to focus on the use of the damper pedal to prevent the piece from losing clarity. In general terms, this composition is truly charming: The melody played with the right hand attracts attention, while the left hand contributes ornaments and the occasional chord.

Musical Style: Studies

- **Composer:** Telfer, Nancy.
- **Work:** "Halley's Comet."
- **Source:** Space Travel, RCM Studies Level 7.
- **Characteristics and purpose:** This composition is made up of massive chords; chords of four notes in each hand until the melody is introduced. Effective use of dynamic bows and pedals is essential.

Technical Studies

Mastery of accented passing notes and major and minor tonalities:

- Specific exercises: Included are exercises designed to perfect the technique of accented passing notes, which are notes that do not belong to the scale but are used to enrich harmony and musical expressiveness. These exercises focus on the precise and fluid execution of these notes within the tonal context.

- Exploring varied tonalities: Exercises also cover a wide range of major and minor keys, including less common ones, to expand the student's understanding and technical proficiency in different tonal contexts.

Introduction to transposition for horn in F:

- Development of transposition skills: Specific exercises and practices are presented to develop the student's transposition skills. This involves the ability to play a piece in a different key, such as the horn in F, which improves the flexibility and adaptability of the performer to different musical situations.

- Understanding music in different keys and registers: In addition to transposition, a deep understanding of how music changes when transposed into different keys and registers is encouraged. This helps the student to have a more complete view of the music and to develop a more informed and versatile interpretation.

Theory and Auditory Training

Study of the structure and forms of classical symphonies:

- In-depth analysis of symphonic forms: This study involves a detailed analysis of the structure of classical symphonies, including their sonata form, rondo, theme, and variations, among others.

- Improved comprehension and performance: By understanding the structure and forms of classical symphonies, students improve their ability to perform these works in a more informed and expressive manner. This enables them to highlight key structural elements and convey the composer's intent more effectively.

Understanding accented pitch notes and their application in melodic writing:

- Exploring the function of accented passing notes: The function and purpose of accented passing notes in melodic writing are studied in depth. These notes, which do not belong to the actual key but are used to create tension and movement in the melody, are explored in different harmonic and stylistic contexts.

- Creative application in composition and performance: Students learn to creatively apply accented pitch notes in the composition of melodies and performance of musical works. This includes understanding how these notes affect melodic direction, harmonic tension, and the overall expressiveness of the music, which enriches both musical writing and performance.

These advanced studies in level 7 of the RCM Program not only broaden students' theoretical knowledge but also foster their creativity and interpretive skills by exploring symphonic structures and accented passing notes in depth.

Musical Dexterity

In level 7 of the RCM Program, musicianship focuses on technical mastery, musical expressiveness, deep analysis, and the ability to perform in unique and creative ways, preparing students to tackle advanced and challenging repertoire with confidence and artistic excellence.

Weekly Sample Practice Schedule

Main Objectives

- mastery of early advanced repertoire

- improvement of technical and expressive skills

- in-depth study of music theory and aural analysis

Time Distribution:

Repertoire and Works

- Early advanced repertoire: 60 minutes.

- Detailed interpretation and in-depth analysis: 20 minutes. A focus on expressiveness, technique, and musical understanding is recommended.

Technical Studies

- Mastery of accented pitch notes and advanced tonalities: 30 minutes. Specific exercises are recommended to develop technical accuracy and fluency in less common keys.

- Transposition practice for horn in F: 10 minutes.

Theory and Auditory Training

- Analysis of advanced harmonic structures and modulations: 20 minutes. A detailed study of music theory applied to the selected repertoire is recommended.

- Understanding and labeling complex chords: 10 minutes.

Musical and Artistic Skills

- Refinement of posture, hand position, and fingering control: 20 minutes.

- Dynamics and musical expression practice: 20 minutes.

- Focus on expressiveness and artistic interpretation of the works.

Breaks and Review

- short breaks between sessions: 10 minutes

- review and consolidation of what has been learned: 20 minutes

Total Practice Time: 3 Hours Per Week

Additional Resources

- Collections of sheet music containing works representative of level 7, including sonatas, suites, preludes, and other pieces by composers, such as Beethoven, and Bonsor, among others. These works should be challenging and varied in style to provide a complete musical experience.

- *The Art of Piano Playing* by Heinrich Neuhaus.

- *Piano Technique* by Walter Gieseking.

- *Harmony and Voice Leading* by Edward Aldwell and Carl Schachter.

Level 8

Level 8 is a crucial point in piano training, marking the transition to a more advanced repertoire and deeper technical and theoretical skills. It is a stage of consolidation and preparation for the advanced level.

Key Topics

- In-depth understanding of stylistic periods: The study focuses on Baroque, Classical, Romantic, and 20th-century styles, exploring the distinctive characteristics of each period and their influence on piano music.

- Exploration of medieval and Renaissance music: Musical concepts and styles from earlier periods are introduced, including Gregorian chant, Renaissance polyphony, and medieval liturgical music.

- Development of advanced technical skills: Work is done on the independence of the hands, the execution of virtuoso passages, expressive interpretation, and control of dynamics and timbre.

Repertoire

Musical Style: Baroque

- **Composer:** Händel, George Friedrich.

- **Work:** "Gigue, Suite No. 7 in G minor, HWV 432."

- **Source:** Piano Suites 1720, imslp.org.

- **Characteristics and purpose:** In a typical Baroque dance suite, the Gigue was presented as the last dance. It is a dance full of life and is performed in a 12/8 time signature. It is replete with rhythmic figures that bring diversity and jubilation. Take time to identify where to place articulations and embellishments that are not specified in the score.

Musical Style: Classical

- **Composer:** Beethoven, Ludwig van.

- **Work:** Six variations on a Swiss folk song, WoO 64.

- **Source:** Variations for piano vol. I, imslp.org, RCM Repertoire Level 8.

- **Features and purpose:** The structure of themes and variations is really entertaining. You could say it's like a compilation of six short compositions—besides the main theme—each one different from the previous one. You'll find triplets, an attractive melody, polyphonic interpretation, and much more.

Musical Style: Romantic

- **Composer:** Liszt, Franz.

- **Work:** "Consuelo no. 1, p. 172."

- **Source:** Consolations S. 172, imslp.org.

- **Characteristics and purpose:** The *Primer Consuelo* is a slow, expressive piece with a choral feel; it is important to play the harmonic intervals at the same time and to emphasize the main melody.

Musical Style: 20th Century

- **Composer:** Satie, Eric.

- **Work:** "Gymnopédie no. 1."

- **Source:** Three gymnopédies, imslp.org.

- **Characteristics and purpose:** This is a lovely piece with deep chords. Its slower tempo makes it more approachable for students. The main challenge lies in handling the wide leaps of the low chords in the left hand. Any of the three gymnopédies can be played at level 8.

Musical Style: Modern

- **Composer:** Peterson, Óscar.

- **Work:** "Jazz Exercise No. 2."

- **Source:** Exercises, minuets, studies, and jazz pieces for piano, RCM Repertoire Level 8.

- **Features and purpose:** Oscar Peterson is recognized as one of the most outstanding jazz pianists in history. In his works, you will find scale figures, arpeggios, and fast, though not chordal, movements. It is important to have a good command of swing-8vos before tackling this piece.

Musical Style: Studies

- **Composer:** Grieg, Edvard.

- **Work:** "Pajarito, op. 43 no. 4."

- **Source:** Lyric Pieces, imslp.org, RCM Studies Level 8.

- **Features and purpose:** This high-speed étude really evokes the feeling of a bird. Fast 32 notes are presented in both hands, interspersed with chirps of 8 dotted. It is a very entertaining imitative piece.

Technical Studies

- Advanced understanding of hybrid time signatures: Reading and performing in unusual time signatures such as 5/4, 7/8, and 10/16 are practiced, developing the ability to maintain a stable and expressive rhythm in these time signatures.

- Advanced rhythm and scale notation: You learn to notate complex rhythms, including compound intervals and syncopations, as well as to write scales with and without key signatures in different keys and modes.

- Mastery of compound intervals: Work is done on the identification and execution of intervals beyond the octave, such as ninths, tenths, and so on, developing aural and technical precision in interpretation.

Theory and Auditory Training

- Detailed study of the history of music: The main stylistic periods are studied in depth, exploring the evolution of music over the centuries and its cultural and social contexts.

- Development of advanced aural skills: The identification of intervals, chords, and complex musical structures is practiced, as well as the aural transcription of pianistic and musical works of other instruments.

Musical Dexterity

In level 8 of the RCM Program, musical proficiency focuses on achieving an advanced level of expressive interpretation and piano technique. Students must demonstrate precise technical control and fluency in virtuosic passages, along with a thorough understanding of the musical structure and interpretive style of the works. This includes the ability to adapt to different musical styles and periods, as well as develop solid memory and concentration skills to perform complex works with artistic excellence and deep musicality.

Weekly Sample Practice Schedule

Main Objectives

- advanced technical and expressive mastery

- deepening of musical understanding and interpretation

- development of an artistic and creative interpretation

Time Distribution:

Repertoire and Works:

- advanced works—level 8 repertoire: 60 minutes

- review and consolidation of learned works: 20 minutes

Technical Studies

- Advanced technical exercises: 30 minutes. Includes chromatic scales, extended arpeggios, and advanced fingering exercises.

- Work on technically challenging passages of the repertoire works: 20 minutes

Music Theory and Analysis

- In-depth analysis of the works performed: 20 minutes. It is recommended to study harmonic structures, musical forms, and interpretative elements.

- Understanding of advanced music theory: 20 minutes. Includes modulations, advanced harmonization, and composition techniques.

Artistic Interpretation Focus on expressiveness and musical phrasing: 30 minutes. Work on dynamics, articulations, nuances, and emotional expression in interpretation.

Review and preparation for presentations:

- review and final adjustments to interpretations: 20 minutes

- preparation for public presentations or exams: 30 minutes

Total Practice Time: 4 Hours Per Week

It is important to maintain a balance between technique, theory, and musical expressiveness to achieve an outstanding level of interpretation at this advanced level.

Additional Resources

- Both of the following offer profound insights into piano technique and expression:
  - *Piano Technique* by Walter Gieseking
  - *The Art of Piano Playing* by Heinrich Neuhaus

- Sheet music collections containing challenging and diversified repertoire for level 8, including works by composers such as Liszt, Peterson, Handel, and others representative of different musical styles and periods.

- *Harmony and Voice Leading* by Edward Aldwell and Carl Schachter.

- *Twentieth-Century Harmony* by Vincent Persichetti.

In conclusion, this chapter has sought to provide a comprehensive guide for those wishing to embark on the journey of learning piano through the RCM Program. From the technical and theoretical basics of level 1 to the complexities and challenges of level 8, we have explored the progressive development of key musical skills. The purpose of this guide is to provide a clear and detailed structure for students and teachers alike, facilitating the process of musical learning and growth. It is hoped that this information will be of use to all those who wish to improve their piano skills and deepen their understanding of music. With this in mind, the transition to the next chapter on musicianship promises to further expand our understanding and appreciation for the art of the piano.

Part III

Beyond the RCM Curriculum

In this part, we will delve into an exciting and enriching topic: exploring diverse musical styles beyond the Royal Conservatory of Music (RCM) curriculum. We will venture into the realms of rock, jazz, pop, and folk music, uncovering the vast landscape of musical diversity and its cultural significance.

You will discover how these varied styles can enhance your musical experience and broaden your cultural horizons. Have you ever wondered how to incorporate these genres into your RCM studies? This section will provide you with the insights and strategies to seamlessly integrate them into your learning journey.

Let's continue on this musical adventure, opening new doors of creativity and inspiration along the way!

Chapter 10

Exploring Different Musical Horizons

Do you ever feel that the rigidity of the Royal Conservatory of Music Program limits your ability to explore alternative musical genres that appeal to you? Do you find yourself enjoying your RCM training but craving additional musical diversity? If so, this chapter is designed specifically for you.

In the following sections, we will enter into a musical expedition that transcends the confines of the program. Our destination is the fascinating universe of jazz, rock, pop, and folk music and how these genres can both enrich and expand your musical repertoire. We'll provide you with a variety of resources, from method books to online courses, to help you dabble in these popular genres.

But that's not all. We'll also equip you with strategies for finding a healthy balance between the structured approach of the RCM and your personal musical interests. Plus, we will teach you how to integrate these popular genres into your classical studies without losing focus.

So, are you ready to unleash your musical creativity and diversify your repertoire? If so, we invite you to read on. This chapter will provide you with the necessary tools to achieve an optimal balance, fostering a complete and enriching musical experience.

A World of Music Awaits You

The Royal Conservatory of Music (RCM) focus on classical music isolates itself from the broader world of keyboard music. A full piano path should not ignore popular genres, such as jazz, rock, pop, and folk music. In this musical journey, we explore these genres and discover how they can enrich your artistic experience.

Expansion of Musical Knowledge By venturing beyond the classical scores, you will discover new harmonies, rhythms, and structures. Each genre has its own history and cultural context, which will enrich your overall understanding of the music. Did you know that jazz was born on the vibrant streets of New Orleans, while pop has transformed over decades of musical evolution?

New Skills Development   Each musical style presents unique challenges. For example, jazz requires improvisational skills, while pop music focuses on catchy melodies and accessible structures. By addressing these challenges, you will improve your technical and expressive skills. Are you ready to improvise over seventh chords in a jazz solo or create a memorable vocal line in a pop song?

Engaging Experience   Monotony can affect even the most passionate musicians. Playing a variety of genres keeps your practice exciting and motivating. Imagine alternating between the smooth chords of jazz and the power chords of rock. Diversity will help keep your passion for the piano alive.

Exploration of Personal Creativity   By immersing yourself in different genres, you'll also have the opportunity to express yourself in unique ways. How about composing a pop ballad with jazz influences? Or fusing folk elements with modern harmonies. Creativity flourishes when we cross musical boundaries.

Focusing on Chords

In contemporary music, chords serve as the fundamental building blocks, forming the harmonic backbone of most songs across genres such as jazz, rock, pop, and folk. Understanding and playing chords allows musicians to grasp the structure of a piece, facilitating easier learning and more expressive performance. For students of classical piano, focusing on chords can offer significant benefits. It enhances their harmonic understanding, supports improvisation skills, and enables them to adapt and create their own arrangements of modern music. By focusing on chords, classical pianists can broaden their repertoire, improve their ability to play by ear, and become more versatile musicians capable of navigating both classical and contemporary musical landscapes.

Understanding chords and their progressions helps pianists grasp the underlying harmonic structure of a piece, making it easier to analyze and interpret the music. Learning chords provides a foundation for improvisation. Pianists can create spontaneous variations and embellishments, adding personal expression to their performances. With a strong knowledge of chords, classical pianists can adapt and arrange modern songs, creating their own versions of popular music. Focusing on chords helps pianists develop the ability to play by ear, identifying chord progressions and melodies without relying solely on sheet music. Mastering chords makes pianists more versatile, allowing them to transition seamlessly between classical and contemporary styles.

Chords are taught rather late in the regular kids program as small kids have smaller hands to make the chord shapes and chords require more theory early on. The focus on chords encourages playing by ear, allowing students to pick out chord progressions and melodies without needing sheet music. You can also work on improvisation by creating your own melodies over known chord progressions. This approach is particularly useful for those interested in playing popular music, composing, improvising, or accompanying other musicians.

Here you would learn the basic three-note chords, inversions, the sevenths chords, and extensions. You learn what chords go with each major scale and then later modes. Learn the Nashville Notation or Roman numerals analysis. Cover basic chord progressions commonly found in popular music, such as I-IV-V, I-V-vi-IV, and ii-V-I. Learn to use lead sheets and chord charts. Learn the basic rhythmic patterns for the left hand, such as arpeggios, broken chords, and block chords.

By focusing on these areas, pianists can develop a comprehensive understanding of chords and their applications, significantly expanding their musical horizons and enhancing their overall musicianship. Whether you are a classical pianist looking to delve into contemporary music or a beginner eager to explore the piano, mastering chords is an essential step in your musical journey.

Beyond Solo Piano Music

The core repertoire of the RCM Piano program consists solely of original music written for solo piano. This focused selection excludes piano or keyboard parts written as part of a band or ensemble, arrangements of other composers' music, works written with lyrics, and keyboard introductions to songs or solos.

In the main repertoire, you will not find the works of notable pianists, keyboardists, and organists such as Keith Emerson, Rick Wakeman, Jon Lord, Ray Manzarek, Jordan Rudess, Herbie Hancock, Chick Corea, Billy Preston, John Lennon, Paul McCartney, Freddie Mercury, Matthew Fisher, Tony Banks, Joe Zawinul, Elton John, Chris Martin, Rick Wright, Jan Hammer, George Duke, Ian Underwood, Patrick Moraz, Dave Stewart, Billy Joel, Mark Kelly, Stevie Wonder, Vangelis, Jerry Lee Lewis, Little Richard, Bill Evans, and Keith Jarrett, to name just a few.

While a select few songs by these artists have been arranged and included in the Popular Selection Lists, the vast treasure trove of contemporary keyboard music remains largely excluded from the formal curriculum. This exclusion presents two main issues: Including contemporary works requires extensive handling of copyright issues, which can be complex and costly. Many contemporary keyboard parts and solos are too short or sporadic to fit the structured requirements of graded material used for examinations.

As a student myself, I—Jamie—wish there was a resource that graded material from these contemporary artists based on performance ability rather than suitability for exams. Such a resource would greatly help with motivation by showing students what contemporary works become accessible as they progress to the next grade. This would be beneficial even if the sheet music were not included, as it would provide clear goals and milestones for students interested in contemporary music.

The RCM's focus on original solo piano music also leaves out solo piano arrangements of orchestral works, including contemporary film scores. In addition, film score adaptations for solo piano are available from renowned composers such as Hans Zimmer, John Williams, and Howard Shore. These adaptations bring the grandeur of orchestral and cinematic music to the solo piano, offering a rich and varied repertoire for students seeking to explore beyond the traditional classical canon.

Supplementing with Other Graded Collections

When looking to expand your piano repertoire, graded collections are an excellent resource. These collections are carefully curated to match specific skill levels, making it easier to find pieces that are both challenging and enjoyable. Here are some of the best options to consider:

Christopher Norton has created a comprehensive series of over 180 original pieces that are graded and suitable for students looking for an alternative or supplement to classical music. Initially published by the RCM through Frederick Harris Publishing, these pieces are now available through Norton's own company. The series spans from a preparatory level to Level 10 and features pieces in popular styles. Additionally, Norton's long-running Microjazz series includes graded material incorporating blues, rock 'n' roll, reggae, and jazz styles.

Martha Mier's Jazz, Rags & Blues series comprises five books of original solo pieces designed for late elementary to early advanced-level students. These pieces are rooted in jazz styles, offering a delightful change from traditional classical repertoire. Mier also has companion series featuring Christmas music, classical themes, and duets, providing a rich variety of pieces for students to explore.

Chester Music offers a series of graded piano solos that blend classical and contemporary styles. These collections cover grades 1 to 5 and provide a diverse range of pieces, making them suitable for students who wish to explore different genres within their skill level.

Trinity College London provides an alternative to traditional classical exams with their Rock & Pop Keyboards series. This series focuses on the performance of three songs to a backing track, with a syllabus ranging from initial to grade 8. Each grade includes a songbook with eight songs, from which students can choose their three performance pieces.

RockSchool offers three series of graded materials: Contemporary Piano, Keys, and Classical Piano. These collections range from debut to grade 8, with each level containing at least six pieces. These collections are designed to cater to students interested in contemporary and classical piano music alike.

The ABRSM has a Pop Performer: Piano series, featuring two books. Book 1 covers pieces from initial to grade 3, while Book 2 includes pieces for grades 3 and 4. This series provides a focused selection of popular music pieces suitable for beginner to intermediate students.

Beyond their lesson books, Faber and Faber offer a wide variety of supplementary books organized in the "Time" series: PreTime (primer), PlayTime (Level 1), ShowTime (Level 2A), ChordTime (Level 2B), FunTime (Level 3A-3B), and BigTime (Level 4+). These series include books on Music from China, Disney, Hits, Popular music, Christmas, Classics, Favorites, Rock n' Roll, Jazz & Blues, Kids Songs, Hymns, and Ragtime & Marches, offering a diverse range of repertoire to suit various interests and skill levels.

New Age piano music is often omitted from structured programs because the pieces tend to be too long relative to their level of difficulty. However, for those interested, Ludovico Einaudi has two collections of graded pieces: one for preparatory to grade 2, and another for grades 3-5. Other notable composers in this genre include Philip Glass, whose pieces range from late elementary to early intermediate levels, and Michael Nyman and Yiruma, whose works are suitable for intermediate to early advanced students.

Graded collections provide a structured and enjoyable way to expand your piano repertoire. Whether you are interested in popular music, jazz, classical, or contemporary styles, there are numerous options available to suit your tastes and skill level. These collections not only supplement your current studies but also offer excellent material for sight-reading and exploring new genres, helping you to become a more versatile and well-rounded pianist.

Jazz

Jazz is a musical genre that developed primarily in the African-American communities of New Orleans, Louisiana, in the late 19th and early 20th centuries. It combines elements of ragtime, blues, and European music. Some of its distinctive characteristics are syncopated rhythms, polyphony, improvisation, intentional pitch deviations, and the use of original timbres. This genre has evolved over time, passing through several distinctive phases of development.

Ragtime was one of the earliest styles of jazz piano, characterized by its syncopated rhythms and lively melodies. Scott Joplin, known as the "King of Ragtime," was a significant figure during this period, with compositions like "Maple Leaf Rag" becoming staples of the genre.

Stride piano emerged from ragtime, featuring a more complex and improvisational style. Pianists like James P. Johnson and Fats Waller were pioneers of stride, known for their virtuosic left-hand technique that alternated between bass notes and chords.

The swing era saw the rise of big bands, where pianists played a crucial role in both rhythm sections and as soloists. Duke Ellington and Count Basie were prominent bandleaders and pianists, each contributing significantly to the development of jazz.

Boogie-woogie was another important style during the swing era, characterized by a repetitive, driving left-hand bass pattern. Pianists like Meade "Lux" Lewis and Albert Ammons popularized this energetic style.

The 1940s brought a radical shift with the emergence of bebop, a fast-paced and complex form of jazz. Pianists like Thelonious Monk and Bud Powell were key figures, known for their intricate melodies, sophisticated harmonies, and improvisational prowess.

The 1950s saw further evolution with post-bop and modal jazz. Bill Evans played a pivotal role in developing a more introspective and harmonically rich approach to jazz piano, particularly through his work with the Miles Davis Quintet.

Cool jazz emerged as a more relaxed and smooth alternative to bebop. Pianists like Dave Brubeck, with his use of unusual time signatures in pieces like "Take Five," and Lennie Tristano, known for his innovative harmonic ideas, were central to this movement.

Hard bop developed as a reaction to cool jazz, incorporating elements of blues, gospel, and R&B. Horace Silver and Art Blakey's Jazz Messengers were prominent exponents, with Silver known for his catchy, blues-infused compositions.

The 1960s saw the rise of free jazz, characterized by its lack of fixed harmony and rhythm. Pianists like Cecil Taylor pushed the boundaries of jazz with their highly energetic and unconventional playing styles.

Avant-garde jazz continued to explore new territories, with pianists like Herbie Hancock and Chick Corea blending jazz with elements of classical music, rock, and electronic music.

The 1970s introduced jazz fusion, combining jazz improvisation with rock, funk, and electronic music. Artists like Herbie Hancock and Chick Corea were instrumental in this movement, with Hancock's "Headhunters" and Corea's "Return to Forever" being landmark albums.

The 1980s and 1990s saw a resurgence of interest in bebop and hard bop, with pianists like Wynton Marsalis and Brad Mehldau leading the way. Mehldau, in particular, is known for his innovative approach, blending classical influences with jazz.

In the 21st century, jazz continues to evolve with pianists like Robert Glasper and Hiromi Uehara, who incorporate elements of hip-hop, R&B, and electronic music into their playing.

Incorporating Jazz Elements in RCM

Jazz, with its rich history and expressiveness, can significantly enrich music practice at the Royal Conservatory of Music (RCM). Here are some clever ways to incorporate elements of jazz:

- Improvisation: Jazz is famous for its improvisation. Instead of strictly following sheet music, students can explore improvisation in their pieces. This not only develops creativity but also improves understanding of harmony and musical structure.

- Jazz repertoire: Introducing compositions by Duke Ellington or Thelonious Monk into lessons can open up new perspectives. These works challenge conventions and offer opportunities to explore syncopated rhythms, extended chords, and expressive melodies.

- Scales and arpeggios: Instead of simply playing scales and arpeggios mechanically, students can apply jazz concepts. For example, experimenting with pentatonic scales, modes, and seventh arpeggios can enrich their technique and harmonic understanding.

Recommended Books

- *The Jazz Piano Book* by Mark Levine: A complete manual for jazz pianists
- *How to Play Jazz Piano* by Jimmy Amadie: Practical approach to learning to play jazz piano
- *Hal Leonard Jazz Piano Method Book 1* by Mark Davis
- *Jazz Piano Foundations* by Jeremy Siskind
- *Exploring Jazz Piano* by Tim Richards

Online Courses

- Udemy: Offers various jazz and piano courses for different skill levels.

- JazzPianoOnline: Features in-depth courses on all aspects of jazz piano. Covers chords, improvisation, theory, and more.

- Berklee Online: Their jazz piano course addresses essential techniques for jazz pianists, such as chords, voicings, improvisation, and more.

Rock

The piano's role in rock music can be traced back to the blues and boogie-woogie styles of the early 20th century. Artists like Meade "Lux" Lewis and Albert Ammons laid the groundwork with their energetic, rhythmic playing, which became a staple in rock and roll.

The syncopation and improvisation techniques from jazz also influenced rock piano. Pioneers like Fats Waller and Count Basie contributed to the development of a more rhythmic and dynamic piano style.

As rock and roll emerged in the 1950s, the piano became a central instrument. Pioneers like Jerry Lee Lewis and Little Richard brought the piano to the forefront with their electrifying performances and high-energy playing. Hits like "Great Balls of Fire" and "Tutti Frutti" showcased the piano's ability to drive the music forward.

The church and gospel music also had a significant impact on early rock and roll. Artists like Ray Charles combined gospel's soulful expressiveness with the driving rhythms of rock and roll, creating a unique sound that influenced many rock pianists.

The 1960s saw the rise of British rock bands like The Beatles and The Rolling Stones, who incorporated piano into their music. Paul McCartney and Billy Preston were notable contributors to The Beatles' sound, with Preston often referred to as "the Fifth Beatle" for his contributions on tracks like "Get Back."

Progressive rock bands like Yes, Genesis, and Emerson, Lake & Palmer pushed the boundaries of rock music with complex compositions and virtuosic playing. Keith Emerson and Rick Wakeman were key figures in this movement, known for their technical prowess and use of synthesizers.

The 1980s saw the rise of electronic music and the widespread use of synthesizers. Artists like Depeche Mode, New Order, and Duran Duran incorporated electronic keyboards into their rock music, creating a new, modern sound. Synth pioneers like Herbie Hancock also blended rock with electronic elements in innovative ways.

The 1980s saw the rise of electronic music and the widespread use of synthesizers. Artists like Depeche Mode, New Order, and Duran Duran incorporated electronic keyboards into their rock music, creating a new, modern sound. Synth pioneers like Herbie Hancock also blended rock with electronic elements in innovative ways.

In the 21st century, rock piano continues to evolve. Artists like Coldplay, with Chris Martin's emotive piano playing, have brought the instrument back to the forefront of popular music. Bands like Muse, featuring Matt Bellamy's virtuosic piano and keyboard skills, have pushed the boundaries of modern rock.

Today's rock pianists often blend elements from various genres, including electronic, hip-hop, and classical music. This fusion creates innovative sounds and expands the possibilities for the piano in rock music. Artists like Alicia Keys and John Legend, though more aligned with pop and R&B, also draw heavily from rock influences in their piano playing.

Incorporating Rock Elements into the RCM Program

Integrating rock elements into the Royal Conservatory of Music (RCM) program can provide a well-rounded musical education and appeal to students interested in contemporary genres. Here are some strategies to effectively incorporate rock elements while maintaining the structured approach of the RCM curriculum:

Understanding Rock Fundamentals

- **Chord Progressions**: Teach common rock chord progressions, such as I-IV-V, I-V-vi-IV, and ii-V-I, to help students recognize and play these progressions in various keys.

- **Rhythmic Patterns**: Introduce the typical rhythmic patterns found in rock music, including straight eighths, syncopation, and driving beats.

- **Rock Scales and Modes**: Cover the use of pentatonic and blues scales, as well as modal playing, which are essential for rock improvisation and soloing.

Integrating Rock Repertoire

- **Supplementary Pieces**: Include rock pieces as supplementary repertoire alongside traditional RCM pieces. Songs like "Let It Be" by The Beatles, "Imagine" by John Lennon, and "Clocks" by Coldplay can provide a modern complement to classical studies.

- **Arrangements and Transcriptions**: Use simplified arrangements and transcriptions of rock songs appropriate for various RCM levels. This allows students to apply their technical skills to contemporary music.

Rock Techniques in RCM Studies

- **Power Chords and Riffs**: Teach students how to play power chords and rock riffs, which are fundamental to the genre. Incorporate these techniques into technical exercises and etudes.

- **Improvisation and Soloing**: Encourage improvisation using rock scales and patterns. Provide opportunities for students to create their own solos over simple chord progressions.

- **Articulation and Dynamics**: Highlight the importance of articulation and dynamics in rock music. Practice techniques such as staccato, legato, and dynamic contrasts to capture the expressive nature of rock.

Performance and Ensemble Opportunities

- **Rock Ensembles**: Organize rock ensembles or bands within the RCM program. This gives students the experience of playing with other musicians and understanding the role of the piano in a rock band setting.

- **Recitals and Concerts**: Include rock pieces in recitals and concerts to showcase the versatility of students. This can also motivate students by allowing them to perform music they are passionate about.

Using Technology and Resources

- **Digital Tools**: Utilize digital tools and apps that are popular in rock music production. Encourage students to explore software like GarageBand, Ableton Live, or other digital audio workstations to create and record their own rock compositions.

- **Online Tutorials**: Supplement lessons with online tutorials and videos from rock pianists. This can provide additional inspiration and practical techniques directly from professionals in the genre.

Connecting Rock with Classical Training

- **Harmonic Analysis**: Analyze the harmonic structures of rock songs to show their similarities with classical pieces. This can help students understand the universal principles of music theory.

- **Technique Transfer**: Demonstrate how classical techniques can enhance rock playing. For instance, the finger strength and independence developed through classical studies can improve the execution of fast rock riffs and solos.

Encouraging Creativity and Expression

- **Composition Projects**: Assign composition projects that require students to write their own rock songs or pieces. This fosters creativity and helps students apply their theoretical knowledge in a practical context.

- **Personal Interpretation**: Allow students to bring their personal interpretation to rock pieces, encouraging them to experiment with tempo, dynamics, and phrasing to make the music their own.

By incorporating rock elements into the RCM program, students can enjoy a diverse musical education that bridges classical training with contemporary interests. This approach not only enhances their technical and theoretical skills but also fosters a deeper connection to the music they love, making their learning experience more engaging and fulfilling.

Pop

Pop is a genre known for its catchy melodies, straightforward lyrics, and polished production. As a pianist, you can incorporate pop into your repertoire by learning popular songs—classics like John Lennon's "Imagine" or more recent hits like Ed Sheeran's "Shape of You" are excellent choices.

Adapt pop songs to the piano, creating unique arrangements. Experiment with chords, rhythms, and ornamentation to give them your personal touch. Also, you can improvise over common pop chord progressions, which will help you develop your creativity and skills as a pianist.

Pop music is a broad and diverse genre that has left an indelible mark on the world's musical culture.

The pop piano sound can be traced back to Tin Pan Alley, where songwriters like Irving Berlin and George Gershwin crafted popular songs that became standards. These early compositions set the stage for the development of the pop genre.

The popularity of Broadway musicals and Hollywood films in the early 20th century also contributed to the emergence of pop music. Composers like Richard Rodgers and Cole Porter wrote songs that became widely popular, influencing the style and structure of pop piano music.

The 1970s marked a significant shift with the rise of singer-songwriters who used the piano as their primary instrument. Carole King's "Tapestry" album, featuring hits like "It's Too Late" and "You've Got a Friend," exemplified the intimate and personal style that became popular during this era.

Elton John and Billy Joel were two of the most influential pop pianists of this period. Their songs, such as "Your Song" and "Piano Man," showcased the piano's versatility and ability to convey emotion and storytelling.

The 1980s saw a technological revolution with the advent of synthesizers and digital keyboards. Artists like Michael Jackson and Madonna incorporated these instruments into their music, creating a new pop sound characterized by electronic textures and danceable rhythms. Hits like "Thriller" and "Like a Virgin" featured innovative keyboard parts that defined the era.

The 1980s also popularized the power ballad, with pianists like Richard Marx ("Right Here Waiting") and Phil Collins ("Against All Odds") bringing emotional depth to pop music through their piano-driven ballads.

The 1990s introduced a more diverse and genre-blending approach to pop music. Artists like Mariah Carey and Celine Dion brought powerful vocals and sophisticated piano accompaniments to their music. Songs like "Hero" and "My Heart Will Go On" became iconic pop ballads.

The 1990s also saw the rise of alternative and indie pop, with bands like Radiohead and artists like Tori Amos using the piano to create unique and innovative sounds. Tori Amos's classically influenced playing on albums like "Little Earthquakes" brought a new level of artistry to pop piano.

The early 2000s continued the tradition of the singer-songwriter, with artists like Alicia Keys and Norah Jones achieving widespread success. Alicia Keys's "Fallin'" and Norah Jones's "Don't Know Why" highlighted the piano's enduring appeal in pop music.

The digital age brought a resurgence of electronic and dance-pop, with artists like Lady Gaga and Adele incorporating piano into their music. Songs like Lady Gaga's "Million Reasons" and Adele's "Someone Like You" demonstrated the piano's versatility in both electronic and acoustic settings.

Today, pop piano continues to evolve, blending elements of R&B, hip-hop, and electronic music. Artists like John Legend ("All of Me") and H.E.R. ("Best Part") use the piano to create intimate and expressive pop music that resonates with a wide audience.

Incorporating Pop Elements Into RCM

Take classical pieces and give them a modern twist. You can add seventh or ninth chords to chord progressions. Experiment with different rhythms and accompaniment patterns or introduce improvisation in appropriate sections; for example, you could take a Beethoven sonata and reinterpret it with pop harmonies and a contemporary rhythm.

Practice playing chords in different inversions and positions on the keyboard. This will help you better understand the harmonies used in pop music and apply them to your own playing.

Listen to a wide variety of popular music, from ballads to rock, jazz, and electronic music, to analyze song structures, chord patterns, and melodies. In addition, pay attention to performance details, such as pedal usage, phrasing, and dynamics.

Recommended Books

These books usually include specific fingerings and techniques for playing Pop music:

- *Pop Piano Hits* by Hal Leonard
- *Contemporary Pop Hits* by Alfred Music
- *The Pop Piano Book* by Mark Harrison

Folk

Folk music is a genre that refers to traditional music passed down from generation to generation. Unlike classical music, which has its roots in Western art music and is based on written musical notation, folk music is played or sung by ordinary people, not professional musicians. It is a tradition passed down orally and spans hundreds of years.

The importance of the piano in folk music lies in its versatility. Although not the instrument most commonly associated with folk, the piano has been used to perform and adapt folk tunes. Classical composers have also based some of their pieces on traditional folk music.

Although it is not the main instrument in the genre, its adaptability and tonal richness allow it to contribute significantly to the folk repertoire.

Folk music is rooted in the traditional music of communities, passed down orally through generations. It encompasses a wide range of styles and cultures, each with its own unique characteristics. Many Western folk traditions, including those in the United States, have origins in European folk music. Songs from England, Ireland, Scotland, and other countries have significantly influenced the folk music landscape.

The influx of immigrants to the United States in the 19th century brought diverse musical traditions, which blended to create a unique American folk sound. The Appalachian region became a melting pot of English, Scottish, Irish, and African influences. Instruments like the banjo, fiddle, and piano played a crucial role in the music of this area.

During the Great Depression, folk music saw a resurgence as a form of social and political expression. Artists like Woody Guthrie used folk music to tell the stories of the common people. The mid-20th century brought a major folk revival, with artists like Pete Seeger, Joan Baez, and Bob Dylan leading the way. The piano often accompanied guitar and voice, providing harmonic support and embellishments.

The folk tradition continued with the rise of singer-songwriters in the 1970s, such as James Taylor and Joni Mitchell, who incorporated piano into their introspective and personal songs. Contemporary folk music often blends with other genres, including rock, pop, and country. Artists like Mumford & Sons and The Lumineers have popularized a modern folk sound that includes piano and other traditional instruments.

Incorporating Folk Elements in RCM

Research and learn traditional melodies from different cultures. You can find sheet music or recordings of folk songs. Then, play these melodies on the piano and pay attention to the nuances, rhythm, and typical folk ornamentations.

Explore the characteristic rhythms of different folkloric genres. For example, the joropo in the llanera music of Venezuela or the candombe in Uruguay. Adapt these rhythms to the piano and experiment with chord patterns and arpeggios that reflect the rhythmic essence of the folklore.

Use typical folk scales and modes in your improvisational playing. Create variations on existing folk tunes. And also, add embellishments and rhythm changes to give them your personal touch.

Finally, draw inspiration from stories, legends, or traditions to compose your own pieces. Experiment with chords and harmonic progressions that evoke the atmosphere of folklore.

Recommended Books

Folk Songs for Easy Piano It contains simple arrangements of folk songs.

First 50 Folk Songs You Should Play on the Piano

- This book contains 50 popular folk songs arranged in a simple way for beginner pianists.

- Includes lyrics and melodies so you can learn as you play.

- Some of the songs included are "Amazing Grace," "Buffalo Gals," "Scarborough Fair," and "Yankee Doodle."

English Folk Song Adult Piano Adventures All-In-One Lesson Book 1

- This book is part of the *Adult Piano Adventures* series.

- Provides lessons and suggestions for learning folk songs on the piano.

Finding Balance and Harmony

Music, like a flowing river, requires a delicate balance to maintain its fluidity and beauty. In music education, this balance becomes even more important. How can we find harmony between the rigorous structured curriculum of the Royal Conservatory of Music and our personal interests?

RCM is known for its rigorous approach to classical music education. Students are immersed in the theory, technique, and performance of composers such as Bach, Beethoven, and Mozart. This approach provides a solid foundation and develops essential technical skills. However, it can be overwhelming and limiting if not properly balanced.

The Importance of Musical Diversity

Music is a vast universe with diverse genres and styles. Ignoring other genres would be like looking at only part of the night sky. Here are some strategies for incorporating variety into your music practice:

- Explore different genres: Spend time listening to and studying music outside the classical realm. Jazz, blues, pop, world music: every genre has something to teach us.

- Integrate elements into your practice: Why not play a classical piece with a jazzy twist? Experiment with harmonies, improvisation, and unconventional rhythms.

- Set personal goals: Define your personal musical goals. Do you want to compose, improvise, or play in a band? Align your practice with these goals.

Time management is key to maintaining balance. Here are some strategies:

- Time blocks: Divide your practice into blocks. Dedicate one to classical technique, one to improvisation, and one to exploring new genres.

- Quality over quantity: It's not just about how long you practice, but how you practice. Practice with focus and mindfulness.

But balance doesn't always mean dividing your attention equally. Rather, it's about integrating the classic and the contemporary. Some benefits of this holistic approach are:

- Creativity: The fusion of styles awakens creativity. You can compose a classical piece with modern influences.

- Personal expression: Music is an expression of our soul. Don't limit yourself to one style; let your unique voice come through.

In this chapter, we explored musical horizons with the curiosity of a child discovering a new toy. The RCM Program has taken us through diverse genres and styles, from the classical notes of Mozart to the vibrant rhythms of jazz. Every chord, every scale, has enriched and broadened our musical understanding.

The importance of lifelong learning has emerged as a jewel in our crown of knowledge. As musicians, we never stop learning. Every note is an opportunity to grow, hone our skills, and discover new forms of expression. Music is a never-ending journey, and we are passionate travelers.

And what about the joy of discovering new musical styles? It's like opening a surprise gift. Blues whispers to us stories of wandering souls, while rock makes us jump and roar. Flamenco envelops us in passion and fire, and electronic music takes us to futuristic worlds. Each style has its own voice, and we, as musicians, are melodic polyglots.

And now, dear RCM student, I want to tell you this:

You are the blank score. Write your own notes and create your own melodies. Don't be afraid to stray from the beaten path. The music is yours to explore, shape, and love.

So keep playing and keep dreaming.

Conclusion

Learning to play the piano from scratch or having previous knowledge and returning to it after having abandoned it for some time is a challenge. The first step to face it is to take the decision to do it, and the second is to look for the best method and the adequate tools so that the initial enthusiasm does not wane, and on the contrary, it is maximized with time until the proposed goals are achieved. That is the idea and function of this book. It sets out how to navigate through the RCM Program, made by the Royal Conservatory of Music, a Canadian institution of national and international renown, which has been teaching music for over 130 years and has a highly structured teaching program that has trained world-renowned artists. This program is one of the best methods in the world for teaching music, which leads you with a steady hand to master this beautiful instrument.

Here, we exposed in the most detailed way possible, pleasantly, and simply at the same time, what each level of this program has in store for us in terms of its theoretical part, technique, repertoire, and exams, to face them in the best way, which will make you advance safely and encourage your progress.

Training exercises are proposed, guidance is given in the search for a qualified teacher, and resources specific to the RCM method are recommended. In addition, we encourage you to look for others outside of it in order to broaden your knowledge and musical spectrum with styles that suit your preferences.

This work is based on our personal experiences; we were also in that place full of aspirations and desires in order to fulfill an old desire, but we faced difficulties and questions that put a veil of doubt in our desire to achieve it, not having enough information about this method, so it took us longer than expected to adapt to it and succeed. Therefore, this book is the conclusion of an exhaustive investigation, going to the right sources to provide those who go through its pages with all the information gathered in one place.

Nothing is impossible when we want to make it happen, and the end of the road is always reached by taking the first step. So, don't give up on your dreams, fight to achieve them because the reward is priceless compared to the challenges faced.

We hope this book will be your companion and permanent guide through this path that comes to an end only when you decide. Each piece you play will vibrate in your soul and in every soul that listens to it.

References

Adult piano adventures. (2009) Books 1-2. Dovetree Productions.

Akira ikegami [Video] (n.d.). YouTube.
https://www.youtube.com/@AkiraIkegamiChannel

Alfred's basic adult piano course. Levels 1-3. (1996). Alfred Music Publishing Co.

Babyuk, T. (2020). *RCM piano repertoire - full list of pieces.* Dacapomusic.ca.
https://www.dacapomusic.ca/blog/rcm-piano-repertoire-all-pieces

Boer, R. (2021, January 21). *A guide to technical exercises for piano.* Music Tutor Online.
https://www.musictutoronline.com/post/a-guide-to-technical-exercises-for-piano

Celebrate theory. Preparatory to level 8. (2016). Fredrick Harris Publishing

Celebration series piano repertoire. Book preparatory A to level 10. (2022). Fredrick Harris
Publishing

Celebration series études. Levels 1 to 10. (2022). Fredrick Harris Publishing

Core piano repertoire that every pianist should know. (2020, September 11). PianoLIT.
https://pianolit.com/blog/core-piano-repertoire-that-every-pianist-should-know

Curriculum and disciplines. (n.d.). The Royal Conservatory of Music.
https://www.rcmusic.com/learning/about-the-royal-conservatory-certificate-program/curriculum-
and-disciplines

Digital learning. (n.d.). The Royal Conservatory of Music.
https://www.rcmusic.com/learning/digital-learning

Dijak, V. (2021). *Why is RCM level 5 music theory so important?* Vanjadijak.mymusicstaff.com.
https://vanjadijak.mymusicstaff.com/News---Blog-Posts?PostID=84972

Eliot, G. (n.d.). *George Eliot quotes.* BrainyQuote.
https://www.brainyquote.com/quotes/george_eliot_161679

Four star sight reading and ear tests. Book preparatory A to level 10. (2022). Fredrick Harris
Publishing

Green, P., Wardrop, P., & Higgs, J. (2012). *Royal Conservatory of Music.* The Canadian
Encyclopedia.

https://www.thecanadianencyclopedia.ca/en/article/royal-conservatory-of-musicconservatoire-royal-de-musique-emc

Jack. (2020, January 12). *The complete guide to learning the piano.* Piano Reviewer. https://pianoreviewer.com/complete-guide-learning-piano

Mozart, W. A. (n.d.). *Wolfgang Amadeus Mozart quotes.* GoodReads. https://www.goodreads.com/quotes/49752-the-music-is-not-in-the-notes-but-in-the

Newman, T. (2023). *Étude in music: Definition, history & examples.* Study.com. https://study.com/learn/lesson/ etude-overview-instruments-examples-what-is-a-musical-etude.html

Piano 2022 edition syllabus. (2022). The Royal Conservatory of Music. https://rcmusic-kentico-cdn.s3.amazonaws.com/rcm/media/main/about%20us/ rcm%20publishing/piano-syllabus-2022-edition.pdf

PianoTips [Video]. (n.d.). YouTube. https://www.youtube.com/@pianotips2623

pianoTV [Video]. (n.d.). YouTube. https://www.youtube.com/@PianotvNet

Program overview. (n.d.). The Royal Conservatory of Music. https://www.rcmusic.com/learning/about-the-royal-conservatory-certificate-program/program-overview

RCM (2022). *Piano études series.* Frederick Harris Publishing

RCM online ear training & RCM online sight reading. (n.d.). The Royal Conservatory of Music. https://www.rcmusic.com/learning/digital-learning/rcm-online-ear-training-rcm-online-sight-reading

RCM, what it is and how it can help you. (2023, January 23). PianoLIT. https://pianolit.com/blog/rcm-what-it-is-and-how-it-can-help-you

Rebecca. (2022, December 7). *RCM level 1 piano repertoire, celebration series sixth edition [Overview].* Rebecca's Piano Keys. https://rebeccaspianokeys.com/rcm-level-1-piano-repertoire/

Seger, S. (2021, December 14). *What is musicianship, and why does it matter?* Concord Conservatory of Music. https://concordconservatory.org/what-is-musicianship-and-why-does-it-matter/

Sight reading. (n.d.). The Royal Conservatory of Music. https://www.rcmusic.com/learning/digital-learning/rcm-online-ear-training-rcm-online-sight-reading/sight-reading

Technical requirements for piano. Preparatory to level 8. (2015). Fredrick Harris Publishing

The Royal Conservatory of Music: A certificate program. (n.d.). Encore. https://www.encoremusicacademy.net/royal-conservatory-of-music-certificate-program/

Theory syllabus. (2016). RCM Publishing.

Trevor. (2021, January 27). *280 Technical exercises for level 1 piano students.* Teach Piano Today. https://www.teachpianotoday.com/2021/01/27/280-technical-exercises-for-your-level-1-piano-students/

Van Betuw, A. (2020) *Design your piano path: The 6 essential steps to mastering your piano journey.*

YourClassical. (2020). *What is an étude?* ClassNotes. https://www.classnotes.org/story/2020/06/24/what-is-an-etude